T0198669

"Sharon is a phenomenal writer! We were so grateful to read her inspiring words and play a role in sharing them with the world when she contributed to *365 Moments of Grace*. Sharon does a great job of conveying the power of belief and the magic of the universe through her personal experience. We look forward to reading more from her."

Jodi Chapman and Dan Teck
Creators of the bestselling *Soulful Journals Series* and *365 Book Series*

♥

"*Messages from the Heart* was birthed from one woman's deep listening to self and spirit. It highlights that when we are tuned in at a soul level we can trust that our messages will have universal appeal. I celebrate Sharon for sharing her gifts in this beautiful book with the world."

Angela Boyle
Author of *Marvellous Me* and Creator of Being Me Books

♥

"Sharon is one of the most authentic people I have ever had the luck to meet. Her writing is a gift — wise, insightful, often funny, illuminating and transformative. *Messages from the Heart* offers a gentle reminder, of what really matters and a warm invitation, to be your very best self. I can't recommend it highly enough."

Alex Kingsmill *BA/LLB (hons.)*,
GDipCoun&HumServ, MScCoachPscyh.
Founder and Director of Upstairs Coaching

♥

"A chance meeting with Sharon at the aquatic centre reaffirmed my belief that everything happens for a reason. Not only did I find a friend for life with myriad shared interests and beliefs, but we agreed her column was the perfect fit for the city's tri-weekly newspaper. Sharon's insights, hunger for life and positive attitude have never failed to amaze me. She is an incredible woman. Sharon's writing is both insightful and inspiring and I am proud to call her a friend and fellow writer."

Monique Patterson
Digital Journalist and Specialist - *The Standard*
Former Editor of *The Area News*

MESSAGES FROM THE HEART

39 Answers to YOUR Life Questions

Sharon Halliday

BALBOA
PRESS

A DIVISION OF HAY HOUSE

Balboa Press books may be ordered through booksellers or by contacting:

Balboa Press
A Division of Hay House
1663 Liberty Drive
Bloomington, IN 47403
www.balboapress.com.au
1 (877) 407-4847

Because of the dynamic nature of the Internet, any web addresses or links contained in this book may have changed since publication and may no longer be valid. The views expressed in this work are solely those of the author and do not necessarily reflect the views of the publisher, and the publisher hereby disclaims any responsibility for them.

The author of this book does not dispense medical advice or prescribe the use of any technique as a form of treatment for physical, emotional, or medical problems without the advice of a physician, either directly or indirectly. The intent of the author is only to offer information of a general nature to help you in your quest for emotional and spiritual wellbeing. In the event you use any of the information in this book for yourself, which is your constitutional right, the author and the publisher assume no responsibility for your actions.

Any people depicted in stock imagery provided by Thinkstock are models, and such images are being used for illustrative purposes only. Certain stock imagery © Thinkstock.

Print information available on the last page.

ISBN: 978-1-5043-0842-7 (sc)
ISBN: 978-1-5043-0843-4 (e)

Balboa Press rev. date: 06/20/2017

For my husband Stephen and our children Leo and Eva. Thank you for supporting me in pursuing my dreams. Without you none of this would be possible…or worth doing anyway.

"What a gift it is to receive one simple idea that can transform your life forever!"
John F. Demartini
Author of *The Riches Within*

Contents

Foreword

I felt a tap on my shoulder. As I turned around a woman said, "This might seem weird, but my intuition told me to introduce myself to you."

We were attending the 2014 Hay House Writer's Workshop in Sydney. At the time, Sharon Halliday was an aspiring author and I was already a published author with Balboa Press, the self-publishing division of Hay House. I was promoting my new book, *You Are A Wonderful Mother*.

Another attendee, Anna Gaddes, who Sharon had serendipitously met in the elevator that morning, joined us. We agreed to have lunch together.

In a bustling food court, we ate lunch and crammed in as much discussion as we could about our families and writing – two of our great loves.

Sharon eagerly wanted to know how I juggled my writing, my speaking engagements, my triathlons, and my family. I was eager to remind her that her writing would take its course if she kept working at it, but that those early years with your children pass by so quickly…and before you know it the kids are at school. At the time Sharon had a 17-month-old and another child about to start school.

Some months after the workshop Sharon would buy copies of my book for her friends who were also mothers. It reminded me of my own writing journey and how I'd created a book that was inspiring people.

Sharon and I stayed in touch and whenever we talked or emailed, we had this great connection. It seemed as though we could talk for hours and we were on similar paths having similar experiences. She seemed to appreciate my insight and advice about book publishing.

Then on Monday February 23, 2015 I was the first person Sharon called when she discovered that she had missed out on winning a book contract in the Hay House Writer's Workshop competition. The disappointment in her voice echoed through the phone. We discussed her publishing options and by the end of the call we had arrived at the conclusion that this was not the end of her writing. We knew the universe had a bigger plan and now was a time to let go and trust.

One year later, Sharon was writing weekly columns as Ask Sharon for her local paper, *The Area News*. By the end of that year, it dawned on her that she had in fact, created a new book, the one you hold in your hands.

Sharon's writing is inspirational, beautiful, motivational and so from the heart. Through her real-life stories and messages, she gently brings us back to the deep and simple truth in our own hearts. She reminds us that the greatest gift is to love and be loved in return. This book is a true blessing from above. Thank you so much Sharon for sharing it with us.

Now, as she tells me that she plans to attend the upcoming Hay House Writer's Workshop in Sydney – back where we first met, where it all began – it feels as though we have come full circle. This time, maybe someone will tap her on the shoulder.

Grace McClure
Author of *You Are Wonderful Mother*

Introduction

Two mothers, an aquatic centre and a golden opportunity

It all began with a chance meeting in late 2014, which saw me chatting with a mother at our local aquatic centre. As we watched our sons splashing about, we would discover that they were actually best friends at preschool, she and I had just never crossed paths before. I would discover that the mum sitting next to me was the editor of the local newspaper, *The Area News*.

A few questions back and forth and Monique learned that I did angel and oracle card readings as part of my Reiki healing practice, Healing from the Heart. She was intrigued and asked if I would write a weekly column for the Friday edition of the newspaper incorporating my card readings. And the rest, as they say, is history. *(This chance meeting and my ensuing friendship with Monique Patterson is the subject of my last column, number 39 "Don't ever give up on your dreams.")*

The writing begins…

Needless to say, I was excited (and also a little nervous), at the prospect of writing a weekly 350-word column for a newspaper which covered a number of communities, including the city of Griffith. What's more, the format of the column meant that I'd be receiving questions from real people about real-life issues and I would be required to provide some kind of useful advice.

While I was confident in my ability to produce a meaningful card reading that would help people, I was well aware that this was something new and unconventional that hadn't really been done before, at least not in a regional area, and certainly not in this area. And on top of all that, we had only relocated from Batemans Bay to Griffith for my husband's work six months prior.

Despite the ball of emotions I was experiencing, the overwhelming feeling was one of appreciation, sprinkled with relief that I was finally getting an opportunity to pursue my heart's desire of having my writing published. The icing on top was that maybe in the process I would also get to help people with their questions about life.

On the right track

Two days after Monique's proposal, in the early hours of the morning, I began 'receiving' messages about what a first column could include to introduce myself to the community. Later that same morning, an email arrived from Monique suggesting I begin drafting some ideas for an introductory column! This was further confirmation that I was on the right track.

The columns are created

The book you are holding in your hands is the collective edition of all the columns which I wrote under the pseudonym of Ask Sharon. Members of the public submitted questions. They covered everything from work, parenting and relationships to money and health. I then combined my experience as a certified Angel Intuitive and card reader with messages that came to me (at all times of day and night), to offer guidance and insight into the questions people asked. I incorporated some simple, but useful tips based on strategies that I had tried and tested myself which I felt people could apply to their own lives. I dotted my writing with some relevant popular culture references and consulted the best self-help principles and philosophies from around the world. I added in the odd quote from a well-known personality and voila! the columns took shape and were ready for publishing.

Response from the public

After a while, people who knew me and were following the columns, would stop me in the street to comment about how much a piece of writing had resonated with them. Some people opened up about issues they were having that had been the subject of one of the columns. One lady, who I'll never forget, burst into tears when she told me the impact one of my columns about money had on her. She said, "You have changed the way I will think about money now. Thank you." It had clearly been something she had battled with for a while and the relief in her eyes was astounding.

Not without its challenges

It was this positive feedback that kept my motivation high and not once did I miss a deadline or feel as though I couldn't provide an answer. Often my greatest challenge was keeping the material to a reasonable word count based on the space I'd been given for the columns. So I would painstakingly have to cut words without losing the meaning of the answer. My other challenge was finding time to dedicate to writing, as a mum of two and wife to a shift-working partner. But that's where emails to myself at 3am under the covers (so as to not disturb my sleeping husband), came in handy!

"I'm officially a published author!"

My first column was published on December 12, 2014 and my last official column was published on December 11, 2015.

(Although I would do one other follow-up Special Edition column for International Women's Day on March 4, 2016 – see A Final Word). In total, I wrote 50 columns which included several special edition ones for Mother's Day, Father's Day, International Women's Day, the Walk A Mile In Her Shoes campaign and the murder of Stephanie Scott. The latter was undoubtedly the most challenging piece of writing I have ever done. *(See Special Edition: Time to Show Compassion from April 17, 2015.)*

Time for answers

During the year in which I wrote the columns, it became clear to me that the questions being asked had universal appeal – these are things that many of us have wanted to know the answers to, at least at some point in our lives. We are answer-seeking beings – we want to know! Indeed, I too have had to read back over the columns for advice in the search for answers to my own personal questions. And when I found them I would always be met with a sense of comfort and relief – like a huge weight had been lifted from my shoulders.

It is my hope that you will have some of your questions answered here and that you too will be met with many an "aha" moment.

December 12, 2014

Introducing Ask Sharon

ARE you looking for a little guidance in the lead up to Christmas? Sharon Halliday, a new Griffith resident, is a certified Angel Intuitive who offers angel and oracle card readings.

The cards are a light-hearted and playful approach to receiving guidance – and we can all do with a bit of that at times in our lives. Yet they can also have a powerful effect and it is always positive.

The guidance can cover a range of subjects, from relationships to attracting more wealth, to healthy lifestyle changes and discovering your life purpose. Whichever cards are drawn, they are always relevant and accurate. At times, the card readings I have carried out for myself have taken me from utter despair to hopeful and empowered. It is not about placing power outside of one's self but rather having trust that we are always being guided in the right direction. Angel and oracle cards can make that an enjoyable process.

We all have the innate ability to use our intuition. Those gut feelings and inner nudges we receive from within are often guiding us toward something (or away from something) for our greatest good. When it comes to conducting card readings, I have simply learned to tune in and trust my feelings to guide the cards and the answers people are seeking. While I can appreciate my personal ability to carry out the card readings, I see it as being no different to someone who is good at their job.

Ask anyone on the street, "How are you?" and the most

common response will be "busy", yet many of us have had that feeling or question of whether busy is actually living.

Those thoughts of, "Is this all there is?" can cause us to wonder if what we are doing day by day has meaning. We all want to know that there is a light at the end of the tunnel of whatever we are experiencing in our lives.

As a recovering workaholic, I have turned my attention inwards. While I have always wondered about the mystery of life, my desire is to live to my fullest potential, live my best life – not next year or when the kids go to school, but right now. I have discovered that we all want the same things: love, harmonious relationships, abundance, peace and fulfillment.

We all have similar questions and sometimes we seek the answers by looking outside of ourselves. We have all the answers within and card readings are a way to access those answers.

The most common questions people ask from card readings are:

- ♥ How can I experience more joy and happiness in my life?
- ♥ How can I lose weight/relax/feel good about myself?
- ♥ How can I attract more money/prosperity/abundance?
- ♥ Am I in the right job or career?
- ♥ What is my purpose in life?
- ♥ What do I need to know right now?
- ♥ And then there's the big one: "What is the meaning of life?"

Our true self and the Universe are communicating with us all the time, often through signs. When you find a coin or feather, witness the beauty of a rainbow, see repetitive numbers – they are all messages. It is all about helping you move in the direction of your dreams and higher purpose – your destiny.

We have come to experience joy, beauty, love and peace – not struggle, despair, or discontentment. Angel and oracle cards are another way the Universe can communicate with you, if you are open, if you are ready.

Each week, locals have the opportunity to submit a question for me to tune into and receive advice from the cards.

December 26, 2014

Column 1: Should I stay or should I go?

THIS week Mark asked: "I'm unsure whether to stay in my current job. Lately I'm becoming more frustrated with the actions and decisions of some colleagues. Would it be best to move on?"

When I contemplated this week's column, before I even knew the question, I began receiving strong feelings about its core messages. When I tuned in more acutely and drew the cards in response to your question, this is what they revealed.

The first card *Communicating Freely* symbolises the source of your concern and frustrations. Do you feel you have not been speaking up for yourself? Have you had some great ideas at work but felt unsure of how to express them for fear of others' reactions?

Know that you can speak your truth in a way that is respectful and composed, yet still honours your feelings about the situation. It is about taking a risk and stepping out of your comfort zone. I can assure you this always works out for your highest good, and actually for the good of those around you, even if you can't see it at first. My suggestion would be to heed the advice from the guidebook, "This isn't the time to step back – rather, it is time to step forward and share from your heart."

Mark, please don't let the image of the girl playing her flute with her pet unicorn distract you from the true meaning of this next card: *Following Your Bliss*. This card represents your resolution. It is all about discovering what brings you the most joy. What are you truly passionate about?

You don't need to necessarily leave your job. If you are already in your dream job or are satisfied with your daily work, then the issue might be about not letting your outer circumstances dictate your inner sense of peace and wellbeing. Easier said than done…I know.

You can however take small steps toward a new job or career that better fits with your desires and passions. Maybe while you are still in your current job, you can begin exploring other avenues. There might be a part-time course in your preferred field. Once you start to pursue what "makes your heart sing" you will feel energised and re-invigorated. This is a good indication of when you are on the right path. It is possible to combine what you love with your career. When you act from a place of joy, doors of opportunity will fly open for you.

The final card *Being in the Flow* represents a possible future outcome from following the advice of the other two cards. For you, it demonstrates that once you speak your truth and follow your path of joy, you will feel more in the flow.

You may have noticed lately that you have been encountering moments where life feels like a struggle and more stressful than usual. This is an indication that there is an easier way if you take a step back and consider whether you feel you are on the right path. When you are in the flow, life is easy. Signs, insights, and your next action step, present themselves in what seems like miraculous ways. The key is to follow your heart's true desires then you will see how life will unfold more naturally for you.

Today's cards have been drawn from the Gateway Oracle Cards. All material relating to the cards and guidebook is copyright to Denise Linn, 2012.

2

January 9, 2015

Column 2: Time to let go of negativity

THIS week Claire asked: "Once again I've overindulged at Christmas. I usually find it takes me a while to recover. What can I do differently?"

Today I was drawn to Doreen Virtue's *Archangel Raphael Healing Oracle Cards*. The first card was *Forgiveness Heals*. You might think, "What has forgiveness got to do with overindulgence?" But honestly, there could not have been a more accurate card to represent the source of the issue. It is about replacing toxic emotions with peace and health. When you are angry with yourself or others, it is you who suffers. This card symbolises that it is time to let go of past negative experiences and emotions that have been stored in your mind, heart and body. You may be pleasantly surprised by how much physical and emotional baggage you let go of by allowing yourself to forgive.

The second card was *Detoxification*. It doesn't mean you have to buy a program or pills, quite the opposite. A detox can be as simple as refining what and how you eat and drink (without judgement). It can be about moderation as opposed to cutting entire things out. It can be reducing some things you consume and increasing others (you will have an instinct about what these are already). It can be starting your day with some fresh lemon juice in a glass of water to kick-start your metabolism. Do explore what detoxification means to you, but I am getting a strong sense that this card's message will ring true because it is something you have considered for some time.

3

Take it slowly; enjoy the process by looking at it as an act of self-love. When you begin to take care of any aspect of yourself, your effort will be rewarded by how you feel within. The outer effects will be the icing on the cake (no pun intended).

The final card, which can represent the result of acting on the other two, is *Unconditional Joy*. It also highlights that it is possible to attain joy right now regardless of your circumstances. I can see two quick ways to get you on the path of joy. Firstly, give yourself a break from judgement. When you continue a behaviour and then judge or berate yourself for it, you will stay stuck in a dysfunctional cycle. When you acknowledge that what you've been doing in overindulging is an attempt to soothe yourself and fill a void with something (like food or alcohol), you can begin a process of empowerment and be open to positive choices. This will lighten the load and allow joy to re-enter your life.

Secondly, be grateful for everything you have in your life now. You could obtain a nice crystal, but a rock will do. Place it in your pocket and throughout your day when you notice it be thankful for anything and everything you can think of. This can be a powerful practice. You can be thankful for anything from your family or home, to a flower or a breeze.

Today's cards have been drawn from the Archangel Raphael Healing Oracle Cards. All material relating to the cards and guidebook is copyright to Doreen Virtue, 2010.

January 21, 2015

Column 3: Mary seeks advice on life

THIS week Mary asked: "I think I know what to do, easier said than done. I want to wake up and feel alive. I have opportunities, but replace that with a to-do list making my day slip away. Maybe something you say to me may trigger a feeling inside of me to just be."

Mary, you're not alone in feeling this way. We do tend to fill our time with activities that we believe are meaningful. And while some items on our to-do list are in fact meaningful, some we simply can't avoid (the dishes and laundry have to get done sometime right?) But we all have things at times we would rather be doing, personal pursuits, goals and passions that we may not be allocating the time, energy and resources that they deserve – that WE deserve.

When we continue with the mundane and unexciting routines day in day out, it can zap our energy and zest for life. Constant demands competing for our attention often leave us feeling overwhelmed. We think we need a holiday, when really we need balance and to include activities that bring us contentment. Scheduling time just being instead of doing is important too. Quiet time or meditation would help with this.

The *Fulfillment* card has come to you today from Denise Linn's Soul Coaching deck. It features a lady at the centre of a flower with a giant loving heart, symbolising that "alive" feeling you seek.

The message is for you to consider where you are creating happiness in your life. How can you make your existing activities more enjoyable? Can you streamline your domestic duties or delegate some of them to give you more time for fun? You could even give your life a fun makeover. Maybe you have forgotten what it feels like to be elated, blissful, joyous and happy. Sometimes what we need is a good belly laugh. The comedy section of the video store or library can help with that.

If you are unsure of what gives you joy, you could embark on a self-discovery mission. Try new things, explore different past-times and hobbies. Remember it's meant to be fun, it's meant to make you feel happy. And most importantly, know that you're worth it.

Today's card has been drawn from the Soul Coaching Oracle Cards: What Your Soul Wants You to Know. All material relating to the card and guidebook is copyright to Denise Linn, 2006.

January 30, 2015

Column 4: Messages from above

THIS week Louise asked: "I want to believe that the feelings I've had lately are my friends and relatives who have passed, but sometimes it makes me miss them more."

This is an area that is close to my heart, as it is for many. To answer your enquiry, I consulted the *Talking to Heaven Mediumship Cards* by Doreen Virtue and James Van Praagh. I knew that any of their cards would offer you relief, but the one that revealed itself was, *I send you loving signs through nature*. This was the perfect card to bring you comfort and provide clarity for your feelings.

Only recently I was not sure how to interpret signs that I felt were coming from above. I came across a CD featuring a song that played at my friend's memorial, then an old magazine – the cover story featured bowel cancer, which she died from. I knew I could no longer ignore that she was trying to communicate with me. My grief had been blinding me from seeing and feeling her signs.

Sometimes our rational mind gets in the way of our faith. It is our heart that needs to guide us to that inner knowing, especially when we have no tangible proof. It is out of the unknown and unexplainable that our faith is reborn.

When you are feeling doubtful about the validity of signs, ask yourself what brings you more hope? What causes you to feel better? To shut yourself off from the idea that those who are no longer on Earth are connecting with you OR to notice and trust the signs that your loved ones are still with you?

I believe one of the reasons our loved ones pass is because they can be of more service to us in heaven than on earth. I encourage you to be open to the signs. They come to bring you comfort, peace, understanding and guidance.

This passage from the *Talking to Heaven* guidebook highlights the message for you today from your deceased family members and loved ones: "We've sent you birds, dragonflies, butterflies, flowers, clouds, and rainbows. Each time you notice these signs, your body gives you confirmation of who sent them to you."

Today's card has been drawn from the Talking to Heaven Mediumship Cards. All material relating to the card and guidebook is copyright to Doreen Virtue and James Van Praagh, 2013.

February 6, 2015

Column 5: Trust that it will all work out

THIS week Lesley asked: "My life feels like one drama after another. Any advice?"

In nearly every oracle or angel card deck, there is the *Trust* card. And that is the card that has been drawn today from the Osho Zen Tarot. Its commonality indicates the importance of this subject.

So if trust is a word that gets thrown around a lot when it comes to seeking guidance, what does it actually mean?

When you are in the midst of chaos or even a circumstance that you would prefer not to be experiencing, how do you have trust that all will be ok?

The best place to start is by reflecting on times in the past where you have been faced with a challenge and to see with hindsight how it unfolded. If you can say, "I lived to see another day," that is enough. What seemed like a major drama and disturbance at the time became manageable. Sometimes it is through these incidences that we undergo the most learning and growth.

In a blog I wrote about attitude, I suggested that to prevent feeling so out of control in our lives is to "de-mountainise our molehills" – it's about perspective. It can seem difficult at the time, but with practice it gets easier to deal with things as they arise in a more calm and positive manner without getting too ahead of ourselves. Don't play the "what if" game. Sometimes we scare ourselves silly with all the possibilities that often don't eventuate.

When it comes to managing life's curve balls and inciting trust, as clichéd as it sounds, some deep breaths can do wonders. Science shows that regulating our breathing in times of stress enables a relaxation response to help stop the biological changes that occur when we enter fight or flight mode. Oxygen to the brain equals clarity. Then you can work through situations one step, one breath at a time.

Part of today's message for you is to trust your own intuition without question, hesitation or doubt. It's when we second-guess ourselves that all seems to unravel. Trust is about knowing that someway, somehow, everything will work out in the end.

Today's card has been drawn from the Osho Zen Tarot: The Transcendental Game of Zen. All material relating to the card and guidebook is copyright to Osho Zen International Foundation Switzerland, 1994.

February 13, 2015

Column 6: Tap into your own inner truth

THIS week a question was submitted anonymously: "There's nothing wrong with my life but I can't help think there's something more than the daily grind. I'm starting to think I may never realise my dreams. What do the cards have in store for me?"

The card I drew for you is *Inspiration* from Denise Linn's Soul Coaching deck. Interestingly, on the deck's guidebook are the words, "What Your Soul Wants You to Know," so you have come to the right place!

While I feel that you are passionate about aspects of your life including family and friends, even your job, you feel something is missing. Without a sense of purpose and fulfillment, daily life can feel like a grind.

What inspires you? You will know immediately what it is. Often it's during childhood that we form ideas about what we'd like to do and who we'd like to become. As we get older, logic and intellect kick in and we forget about, suppress or deny those dreams that make our soul sing.

When we are inspired, whatever we are doing feels good. Inspiration taps into an inner truth. It's as though electricity is running through your veins. For me, this happens when I write. And it supports my dream of becoming a published author.

It doesn't mean that you have to view your everyday life as boring or separate, quite the contrary. When you create space for inspiration it will cause you to see your existing circumstances with fresh eyes and enthusiasm. That's the effect it has on me.

Incorporating something every day that inspires you is the key. You might start with a few minutes. Over time you will build momentum to do more.

Little by little, day by day, it's those incremental action steps that will bring you closer to your dreams.

As I was considering your question, I came across a 2000-year-old quote by a sage named Patanjali. "Dormant forces, faculties, and talents come alive, and you discover yourself to be a greater person by far than you ever dreamed yourself to be." This is what inspiration will do for you.

Today's card has been drawn from the Soul Coaching Oracle Cards: What Your Soul Wants You to Know. All material relating to the card and guidebook is copyright to Denise Linn, 2006.

february 20, 2015

Column 7 (part one): Respect the key to success

THIS week Catherine asked: "My husband and I are nitpicking at each other more than usual. What can I do to improve the situation?"

Relationships. It's a word that can make us feel all warm and fuzzy or send shivers down our spine!

Around Valentine's Day emotions get stirred up. These occasions can encourage people to reconnect, or highlight problems and unfulfilled needs. Catherine, you've raised a big subject, so I'll be responding in two parts. Next Friday's column will feature another aspect to improving relationships. For today, the *Self-Respect* card from Doreen Virtue's *Archangel Michael Oracle Cards* will bring clarity.

There are few times in life when it's easy to be an individual without others' influence. Perhaps the most significant is when we first leave home and get to explore a sense of freedom.

When we're in relationships, this individualism and freedom can be quashed. We compromise and take into account others' needs, sometimes to our own detriment.

Creating harmonious relationships is about balance and self-respect. When you focus on your own peace and happiness, it naturally has a flow-on effect to others.

I have some suggestions. Do them for you, not solely for the purpose of improving your situation. It's the aeroplane oxygen mask analogy; you can't be present for others until you've put yourself first.

- ♥ Speak your truth (assertively and calmly). Admit the truth to yourself and be willing to make changes. It's not selfish, it's necessary.
- ♥ De-dramatise issues – perspective is a beautiful thing!
- ♥ Trust your instinct (it's rarely about the domestic duties or the kids – these are catalysts for bringing to the surface core issues to be resolved).
- ♥ Focus on the positives – your own as well as what your partner brings to the partnership. As difficult as it seems in the middle of a disagreement, remembering why and how you fell in love in the first place can help defuse some of the tension.

The nitpicking in relationships occurs when resentment builds up. Throw in overtiredness and misunderstandings and you have a classic case of criticism central. It's not about blame on either side. The guidebook sums it up, "This card is a sign that it's time to honour yourself, even if others aren't treating you in a worthy manner."

Today's card has been drawn from the Archangel Michael Oracle Cards. All material relating to the card and guidebook is copyright to Doreen Virtue, 2009.

February 27, 2015

Column 7 (part two): Be kind to yourself and other people

LAST week Catherine asked: "My husband and I are nitpicking at each other more than usual. What can I do to improve the situation?"

The *Self-Respect* card was drawn from Doreen Virtue's *Archangel Michael Oracle Cards*. Today the second part of the answer is about self-love.

Self-love is the mother of all life lessons. When we truly love ourselves we are able to love others wholeheartedly, without conditions or expectations.

Self-love as a concept is nothing new, however, it has become trendy. Recently, it's featured in many newspapers and magazines. As people search for more meaning and balance in their busy lives, self-love is heralded as the way to achieve both, and much more. One could argue that's why we are here – to learn about love – how to receive it, how to give it.

All roads lead back to self-love. Not just relationships with other people but our relationship with money, health and our overall happiness.

Some readers might cringe at the very idea of self-love and that's ok. For many, it's not something that is instilled in them growing up. It certainly wasn't in my case, I am self-love self taught.

I feel more content as a mother, as a wife, as a business owner, as a soul, when I am nurtured and nourished by my own self. It adds value to what I can provide to others.

I'm not suggesting we no longer raise our children and let them fend for themselves, I'm saying that it is healthy for them to see a parent who has the time and energy for them because they are not frazzled, burnt-out and resentful. So, mastering the art of self-love can be as much about inner peace as it can be about an outer legacy.

Self-love takes many forms. This week's suggestions are:

♥ Honouring time and space for yourself – this can create space for others to do the same.

♥ Be aware of the negative self-talk and turn it into a positive – be kinder with your self-judgements and criticisms.

It does take practice, but it has the power to change every aspect of your life. That's enough to make it worthwhile to explore further.

Aristotle said it best, "The most important relationship we can all have is the one you have with yourself, the most important journey you can take is one of self-discovery."

Today's card has been drawn from the Archangel Michael Oracle Cards. All material relating to the card and guidebook is copyright to Doreen Virtue, 2009.

March 6, 2015

Column 8: Appreciate what you have in life

THIS week Sam asked: "I go from week to week when it comes to money. What can I do?"

As a child, one of my favourite songs was ABBA's "Money, Money, Money". I considered it such a playful, upbeat song, I still do. But despite being able to enjoy that song, I grew up with very serious attitudes toward money and working hard for it. Over time, I have lessened my attachment to money and have taught myself to separate struggle from prosperity.

Today, the *Appreciation* card was drawn from the *Money and the Law of Attraction Cards*. Being appreciative is not some airy-fairy principle to take lightly. It is a most powerful way to create an abundant and joyful life.

This is echoed by Esther and Jerry Hicks through the Teachings of Abraham (the authors of today's card): "The fastest way to get to an improved financial condition is to look for pleasing things that you already have."

Cancel out worry by doing whatever it takes to get your mind and emotions in a positive place. Initially, it may seem difficult if worrying is the only way you've known. Take the focus off money. In the very least, it will bring you relief.

Here are my hot tips for showing you the money fast:

♥ Clear the clutter. Space clearing expert Denise Linn refers to it as, "Modern day alchemy. You have to clear out the old to make way for the new."

♥ Avoid talking about money woes and the price of things (it keeps the energy stuck in a place of lack and scarcity).
♥ Notice abundance everywhere – it could be in the form of time, energy or resources.
♥ Use affirmations to change your thinking patterns.

We really do live in an abundant world, if we are prepared to see. Every time I have practiced an attitude of gratitude and been thankful for what I already have, I've received unexpected windfalls, found misplaced money or made savings. It's something you have to experience to believe, and when you do just be sure to say, "Thank you."

Today's card has been drawn from the Money and the Law of Attraction Cards. All material relating to the card and guidebook is copyright to Esther and Jerry Hicks, 2009.

March 13, 2015

Column 9: Don't ignore issues in life

THIS week Caitlin asked: "I'm getting over a breakup, some days are better than others but why do I still feel so sad?"

The *Accepting What Is* card from Denise Linn's *Gateway Oracle Cards* was drawn. While the image depicts a rose in bloom, the messages I received were much more thorny. It seems fitting they coincide with Friday the 13th, which is inherently connected to darkness, for today's message is all about acknowledging the shadow within.

I'm a glass-half-full kind of person, yet I am also acutely aware that negative experiences and emotions do serve a purpose. It is certainly not an enjoyable aspect of the journey but it is a necessary one.

How would we know happiness without having experienced sadness? Courage without fear? Triumph without disappointment? Forgiveness without blame? How would we know the light without having spent time in the dark?

Life is about contrast and experiencing a full range of emotions. To deny them is to deny our whole self.

As spiritual teacher and *New York Times* bestselling author, Marianne Williamson says, "Those aspects of ourselves that we don't like have got to come out in order to be released."

Repressed issues always have a way of rearing their ugly heads…eventually.

So how do you lessen the blow when disappointment, anger, and rejection are ready to go a few rounds?

Tips for embracing your shadow side:

- ♥ Face and clear issues as they arise. It may not be convenient but it saves unnecessary heartache and pain down the track.
- ♥ Don't beat yourself up (still working on this myself!).
- ♥ Realise that even if you can't see the lesson or blessing while you're amidst the challenge, there will be a purpose to it.
- ♥ Remember the old adage, "This too shall pass."

Each one of us will recall a time that we can chalk up as not being our finest moment. Often it's not until later that we can say we learned something from it. Don't curse the experience; clarity is on its way. Accept what is – the good, the bad, the ugly and everything in between. If you can master this approach with your relationships, you'll find it gets easier in every other area of your life.

We all have demons to battle from time to time, but there's no need to go the whole 12 rounds!

Today's card has been drawn from the Gateway Oracle Cards. All material relating to the card and guidebook is copyright to Denise Linn, 2012.

March 20, 2015

Column 10: Embrace life's challenges

THIS week Ken asked: "I missed out on a job I needed so what now?"

I was drawn to the *New Beginnings* card from the *Archangel Power Tarot Cards*.

When something like this happens, it can feel overwhelming. Never mind the disappointment – questions of paying the bills naturally surface. We think we don't have time to stop and take stock. We think we have to quickly move on to the next thing. We consider taking jobs we know we wouldn't like just to keep the dollars rolling in.

Yet, these are the perfect moments to reassess where you are heading and what you want out of life. It can seem unrealistic during a crisis to think of it as a gift or a blessing, but that's exactly what it is.

When you swap doubts and fears for trust and courage, you are tapping into a powerful energy within. You are tapping into the essence of your true self and the answers you seek.

Recently my business was affected by something I had no control over. All I could do was allow the right people with the right expertise to help me at the right time. Meanwhile, I chose to see it as an opportunity to get my house in order… literally. It made me feel better and helped me let go. Then the solution presented itself.

So my new saying is one of Louise Hay's key affirmations, "Everything is working out for my highest good." It provides me with a necessary injection of optimism without the unnecessary details.

Consider these famous words by American writer, Joseph Campbell, "We must be willing to let go of the life we planned so as to have the life that is waiting for us."

Tips for turning obstacles into opportunities:

♥ Trust it will work out for the best – you've landed on your feet before and you will again.
♥ Be open to new directions – pay attention to signs, coincidences and inner nudges.
♥ Swap fear of the unknown for excitement of what could be.
♥ Revisit projects and hobbies that make you feel good - in the very least it will take your mind off worrying.

Before you know it, someone will cross your path seeking your skills and talents and you will wonder what all the stress was about.

Today's card has been drawn from the Archangel Power Tarot Cards. All material relating to the card and guidebook is copyright to Doreen Virtue and Radleigh Valentine, 2013.

March 27, 2015

Column 11: Enjoy every waking hour

THIS week Katy asked: "I worry I'll never find Mr Right. Do you think there's someone for everyone?"

What I share today will be unlike any other relationship advice you've ever heard. It requires an open mind and heart. But it will bring you clarity.

The subject of love is really about vibration. Now, before you go and get all *Fifty Shades* on me, I'll explain. Basically (whether you believe in it or not), the Law of Attraction is always operating. Whichever "vibration" you put out into the Universe with your thoughts and feelings, you get back.

Esther and Jerry Hicks through the Teachings of Abraham explain it further, "Everything that everyone desires…is wanted for only one reason: They believe they will feel better in having it." Relationships are no exception. The key is to feel better within yourself first before the new person can appear.

So the *Following Your Bliss* card from Denise Linn's *Gateway Oracle Cards* is perfect. It depicts a girl playing a flute with a unicorn. She clearly doesn't have a care in the world and is doing what she loves. She epitomises joy. I'm not suggesting you take up the flute (or develop an unhealthy obsession with unicorns), unless that makes you feel happy. The point is that she is happy and free without another soul around.

The irony of this, and getting back to your question, is that when you live from this place of bliss, people want to be around you. You emit a positive "vibration" that is intoxicating and irresistible.

Tips for taking your focus off Mr Right so Mr Right can enter your life:

♥ Place the focus back on you – what makes your inner being happy?
♥ Notice what "vibes" you are emitting.
♥ Let happiness be your aphrodisiac – there's nothing more attractive than a person having fun.
♥ Remember, you may as well feel good on your way to attracting a soul mate.

For many who are ready for companionship and don't yet have it, the waiting game can seem torturous. But it doesn't have to be.

So yes, I believe there is someone (probably several someones), who are a vibrational match to you.

If you follow this advice, you may be so preoccupied with enjoying your life that Mr Right will have to tap you on the shoulder!

Today's card has been drawn from the Gateway Oracle Cards. All material relating to the card and guidebook is copyright to Denise Linn, 2012.

April 10, 2015

Column 12: Treat your body as a friend to lose weight

THIS week Brenda asked: "After having kids I've struggled with my weight. How can I get my body back?"

Self-help literature on weight often suggests focusing on the positives by finding aspects of your body that you *do* like. That might work for some, but I believe the long-term solution lies in our emotions.

We've all heard of emotional eating, but what does it actually mean? I define it as eating for a purpose other than nutrition.

Examining the *why* we eat to comfort and soothe ourselves is one approach (albeit an expensive solution if you go the therapy route). Personally I've found that having an awareness of it and changing my thoughts and behaviours from there has been effective. But I won't sugarcoat it – it takes practice and consistency to develop good habits.

While I am still exploring the inner and outer aspects of body image, what I am sure of is that diet and exercise are only part of the issue – it is as much a spiritual journey as it is a human one.

Thankfully, I stumbled upon a meditation program, *Manifesting True Success* with Deepak Chopra and Oprah Winfrey. In his reference to the body Deepak suggests, "Any time you make a choice about how to deal with your body, ask a simple question, 'Is this how I would treat a friend?' You will immediately know what to do."

Tips for treating your body as a friend:

♥ Notice your emotional triggers for overeating and unhealthy food choices – change begins with awareness.

♥ Consider how you eat – swap devouring for savouring your food and let it delight the senses.

♥ Make yourself number one again. When the kids see mum taking care of herself she gets the body she desires and they get a positive role model, it's a win–win.

You may like to cast aside these suggestions and anything else you've digested on the subject and heed today's card from Doreen Virtue's *Archangel Raphael Healing Oracle Cards*. The one that emerged is *Ask Your Body for a Message*.

After Easter's chocolate overload, now is the perfect time to get in tune with your body and let it guide you back to your true self. If you do that, the number on the scales won't even matter.

Today's card has been drawn from the Archangel Raphael Healing Oracle Cards. All material relating to the card and guidebook is copyright to Doreen Virtue, 2010.

April 17, 2015

SPECIAL EDITION for the Murder of Leeton School Teacher and Bride-to-Be Stephanie Scott: Time to show compassion

My deepest compassion goes to the fiancé, family, friends, colleagues and students of Stephanie Scott. You are in our prayers.

THIS week I won't be answering a question from an individual, I'll be attempting to make sense of the unfathomable event that has been in the minds and hearts of our collective conscience this past week. An impossible task? Probably. Bringer of relief to some? Hopefully.

As I began writing, I was flooded with a heartfelt desire to bring peace and comfort where there has been so much pain, sorrow…and disbelief.

There are many questions that have no answers. "Why should this happen?" produces emptiness rather than explanation.

The inner dialogue that offered a glimmer of light in the dark for me was: "Do tragedies like this encourage us to enjoy the fullness of the precious life we have? Yes. Might we complain a little less about petty matters? I'd like to think so. Does an embrace from a loved one or the words, 'I love you' carry more meaning now? Absolutely!"

I've accepted that we won't be able to get our heads around a tragedy that rips at our hearts like this.

Today I have no practical advice or tips for there are no appropriate words of condolence that could be offered to a family who were planning a wedding and are now preparing a funeral.

Recently I tried to comfort a friend after we had buried a schoolmate, a young mother like us. It was the second friend I had farewelled in as many weeks from cancer. I realised it may have been too soon to utter these words, and once again it may be too soon to share them here, but to believe anything else about death, for me, is untenable.

The words were something to the effect of: "When someone makes their transition through death they re-emerge and realign with the wholeness of who they really are – which ultimately is pure, positive, non-physical, source energy. They never cease to be, for they are eternal consciousness." This reflects my belief on death according to Esther and Jerry Hicks and The Teachings of Abraham. Others refer to death as going home.

By week's end, I arrived at a message from the *Life and Death* card selected from Marianne Williamson's, *Miracle Cards*. "Life is like a book that never ends. Chapters close, but not the book itself. The end of one physical incarnation is like the end of a chapter, on some level setting up the beginning of another."

Our community has been rocked to its very core. Despite the cold hard facts of this case emerging, my heart has been warmed by signs that we are rallying and uniting. My hope is that collectively our spirit will continue to rise, but not in anger, not in hatred for another human being who did an inhumane thing. Can we channel that energy into support, compassion and love for one another?...I know we can.

Today's card has been drawn from the Miracle Cards. All material relating to the card and guidebook is copyright to Marianne Williamson, 2002.

April 24, 2015

Column 13: Releasing yourself from the to-do list

THIS week Joanna asked: "Being busy all the time is getting me down. My friends often feel the same way trying to juggle work and a family. What can we do?"

Why is it that we get ourselves in such a tizz over our to-do list? Is it that constant gnawing sensation or that feeling of drowning that follows us everywhere? Like a juggler with too many balls in the air, eventually they all get dropped. There's no doubting life used to be simpler.

Today there are more demands being placed on us than ever before. Forget the avalanche of advertising bombarding us daily and the emails that breed like rabbits, the reality is that it just doesn't feel good when we think we have to rush quickly from one thing to the next. Even eating in our cars and on the run has become the norm!

My latest go-to gurus on all things life, Esther and Jerry Hicks really make sense on this issue. When it comes to the dreaded to-do list they quite bluntly say, "You cannot ever get it done!" They conclude that because we are an evolving, ever-expanding species, there will always be more to create, to become....and yes, to do.

But before you think I've completely taken the wind out of your sails, I'd prefer you felt as though the pressure-valve has been released. Doesn't it help to know that if we "cannot ever get it done," we might as well have fun along the way?

Tips on how to liberate yourself from the list:

♥ Choosing to do some things well rather than lots of things sparingly will help you to feel less overwhelmed and more fulfilled.

♥ Get acquainted with the Eisenhower Method for determining priorities. Certainly, I was bored out of my brain when we covered this time management tool in school…but it's easy and it works.

♥ Delegate. Be ok with it.

Be gentle with yourself might not be the answer you'd expect, but it is relevant. This *Archangel Michael Oracle Card* by Doreen Virtue is all about giving yourself a break. While you crave a work-life balance, it starts with getting real about what balance means to you. It will be a case of slow and steady wins this (rat) race.

Joanna, now you've got me thinking about my own list. Maybe next time the circus comes to town, I'll add "book tickets" to my to-do. I hope they bring the jugglers!

Today's card has been drawn from the Archangel Michael Oracle Cards. All material relating to the card and guidebook is copyright to Doreen Virtue, 2009.

May 1, 2015

Column 14: Don't sweat small stuff

THIS week a question was submitted anonymously: "I'm usually fairly calm but lately when someone pushes my buttons I feel like I can't control my anger. How can I control it?"

Your question was perfectly timed after a recent spat with my hubby. I knew I had overreacted, I even knew my argument was flawed...but I wasn't ready to admit that yet! While I pondered your question I opened Kristine Carlson's *Don't Sweat the Small Stuff for Women* and like a ray of light the chapter "Speak from Your Love" appeared.

"Why does it become difficult for all of us, at times, to be in touch with the most magnificent part of who we are – our love – and then to speak from this place? Our egos and emotions and habits of reacting and overreacting keep us from speaking from our love. It is most challenging to speak from your love when you are angry."

Is it easy to not respond in anger if that is how you've always handled things? Nope. Can this behaviour be changed? You betcha! As I've said before, when it comes to matters of all things transformation, awareness is king (or queen).

Sometimes the cards reveal a subtle meaning but today it was literal. The *Wait* card from Doreen Virtue and Radleigh Valentine's *Angel Answers Oracle Cards,* indicates the power of a pause, especially in the heat of the moment.

Hot tips for staying cool under fire:

♥ Recognise that there are no winners in a bickering battle. Harmony will most certainly be the first casualty.

♥ Ask, "Is defending being 'right' really worth it?" If you know the truth in your soul is that not enough?

♥ Consider, how good do you really feel after a verbal victory if it's at the cost of another's feelings (or the relationship)?

♥ Remember, there's always room for a hero (or heroine) to emerge.

I heard a touching story in the lead up to Anzac Day about Aussie trumpeter, Sergeant Ted McMahon, who in the middle of battle began playing his cornet. Accounts record the guns on both sides gradually falling silent as he played. It seems the power of a pause can bring peace (even briefly) to a battle on the western front or on the home front.

Today's card has been drawn from the Angel Answers Oracle Cards. All material relating to the card and guidebook is copyright to Doreen Virtue and Radleigh Valentine, 2014.

SPECIAL EDITION for Mother's Day (part one): Show Mum you care on Mother's Day

THIS week the sea of pink and excessive use of the word "special" prompted me to recall conversations I've had with my mummy friends. One of them had asked, "Does Mother's Day really mean anything anyway?"

I began digging. I ended up at Wikipedia (as you do). Mother's Day was founded by American Anna Jarvis to honour her own, and all mothers, as "the person who has done more for you than anyone in the world." When Mother's Day was proclaimed as a national holiday in 1914, it wasn't long before certain card-making companies began cashing in. "Jarvis's intention for the holiday had been for people to appreciate and honour mothers by writing a personal letter, by hand, expressing love and gratitude, rather than buying gifts and pre-made cards."

So what does all this mean to modern mothers? Are they prepared to trade the fluffy slippers and a sleep-in (well, maybe not the sleep-in) for a hand-made card and a "thank you"?

Most mothers embrace the mother of all roles with gusto but somewhere along the way of nappies, nap times and Nanna naps (if we're lucky!) we can lose ourselves. We can even lose our identity, our freedom and for some, our dress sense - flats over heels may no longer be a choice but a necessity.

So what's the key to showing mum how much she is appreciated for her dedication to her family? Sincerity. And it can come in many forms.

Tips on how to uphold the true sentiment of Mother's Day, Jarvis-style:

♥ Help, help and more help but without being asked – *with great gestures comes great recognition!*
♥ Compassion – a little understanding from children and partners can go a long way.
♥ Support her dreams. In Buddhism this is referred to as sympathetic joy. It's a two-way street kind of notion, so let's revisit it when Father's Day rolls around.
♥ Anything you can do to help Mum honour her own needs will be well received (never underestimate the value of uninterrupted bathroom time!).
♥ If in doubt, act from love.

Given the significance of this important relationship and motherhood in general, next week I'll be delving deeper into how mothers can reclaim their sanity and sense of self the other 364 days of the year.

May 15, 2015

SPECIAL EDITION for Mother's Day (part two): Cherish time spent with your child

LAST week I considered the true meaning of Mother's Day and specifically what anyone in a mum's inner circle can do to support them.

This week it's about what mothers can do for themselves to make their busy, demanding lives more enjoyable and fulfilling.

I'm not a fan of hypocrisy so it's critical that anything I write is not only true to my heart but also my experience. This week was no different. Being a mother myself I wanted to present practical pathways to peace that I had tried, tested and would leave a mum feeling triumphant in just about any situation. A big ask, I know!

My quest seemed divinely inspired when I discovered words for the *Totality* card from the *Osho Zen Tarot* deck. It illuminates what mothers can aspire to in order to enjoy the rewarding yet relentless nature of motherhood.

"Developing the knack of being total in responding to whatever comes, as it comes, is one of the greatest gifts you can give yourself. Taking one step through life at a time, giving each step your complete attention and energy, can bring a wondrous new vitality and creativity to all that you do."

Sure, it can be a challenge to appreciate the delight, wonder and joy that comes from motherhood amidst stress, sleep deprivation and squabbles.

So much of what mothers do involves being pulled in different directions; multitasking becomes the norm. Yet, what attentiveness and mindfulness does is encourage us to be fully present in the moment, for ourselves and our families. That means being present for the highs (affection, laughter, fun) the lows (tantrums, demands, fatigue) and even the mundane in between.

Tips on how to balance being you and being mum:

- ♥ Stop trying to control every detail (this has been a biggie for me). Allowing others to be themselves, and giving situations the space to unfold, works out better every time.
- ♥ Drop comparing yourself to other mums; each to their own journey.
- ♥ Release the idea of how you think things *should* be – make acceptance your new best friend.
- ♥ Apply the aeroplane oxygen mask analogy to self-care; in order to take care of others you must first take care of yourself.
- ♥ If all else fails, look into your child's eyes.

Last week, during the Mother's Day service at my son's school, I gained a new perspective on this significant relationship as the words, "Motherhood is a gift" made me stop and think. I considered all the women who are unable to have children, all the mothers who are ill or no longer with us, and closer to home, the friends who I've lost who were also mothers. It dawned on me that despite the challenges, I have been blessed with a gift...time to cherish it.

Today's card has been drawn from the Osho Zen Tarot: The Transcendental Game of Zen. All material relating to the card and guidebook is copyright to Osho International Foundation Switzerland, 1995.

May 22, 2015

Column 15: Take time to enjoy simple pleasures

THIS week Susan asked: "I need a holiday badly but it's not likely to happen anytime soon. Can the cards help me with that?"

What is it exactly about going on holidays that makes us de-stress? Sometimes just the thought of going somewhere different can bring much-needed relief. The whole idea of a holiday is to break away from your usual, everyday routine – nothing like a bit of R&R to recharge the batteries.

In her 2015 bestseller, *Loving Yourself to Great Health*, Louise Hay pinpoints what many of us feel when we are long overdue for a holiday. She says: "We begin to think and feel like we're machines, capable of running nonstop to fulfill a to-do list, and we forget to honour ourselves."

Today's card, *Savouring Pleasure* from Denise Linn's *Gateway Oracle Cards* can help us do just that and indulge ourselves in lieu of a holiday.

Tips on how to bring that happy holiday feeling home:

- ♥ Recreate retreat-like pampering – a long soak in the bath each week can do wonders.
- ♥ Recognise your energy zappers. How can you better spend your time so more can be allocated to meaningful activities that nourish and nurture?
- ♥ Use this as an opportunity to simplify your life.

Dr Travis Bradberry, co-author of *Emotional Intelligence 2.0*, looked at how successful people spent their weekends. Number six on the list was, "They Minimise Chores." Travis reveals how, "Chores have a funny habit of completely taking over your weekends…you lose the opportunity to relax and reflect. What's worse is that a lot of chores feel like work, and if you spend all weekend doing them, you just put in a seven-day workweek."

The solution here is to reschedule chores elsewhere and leave your weekends free – which interestingly is the purpose of a holiday – to feel free.

For many, going on holidays is not just about a break from work but a break from technology (with the exception of the odd selfie). It's the idea of not being contactable and being free to do as you please with spontaneity and without schedules. This is becoming quite challenging as we take our mobile devices everywhere. Consider ways to limit your technology usage – is it one of your energy zappers?

A holiday, like anything else we desire, is something that we believe will make us feel better for the experience of it. The trick is to feel better in the meantime, so that we are not placing our happiness into some external or future goal. Then when the holiday rolls around – and it will – there won't be expectations and pressure for it to be a certain way. All that will be left is for you to enjoy it!

Speaking of enjoying things, I'd better go, I wouldn't want my bath to overflow!

Today's card has been drawn from the Gateway Oracle Cards. All material relating to the card and guidebook is copyright to Denise Linn, 2012.

May 29, 2015

Column 16: Our dreams may contain messages

THIS week Leanne asked: "I have weird dreams. Is there a message in them?"

I'm not a dream expert but Australian author Leon Nacson is. He writes: "It's in our dreams, and the change in rhythm of our minds, that we often tap into emotions that may have been trying to get our attention…Identifying the emotions that pop up in our dreams provides a wonderful opportunity to connect with how we feel, and to better understand where we're at and what is happening in our lives."

The fact that you have enquired about your dreams means you are aware that there is something more to this life, something more than the tangible. I see our dreams as a portal into our true self in the same way that meditation can reveal the answers to all that we seek.

From an intuitive perspective, if your dreams have been "weird" it could indicate that something is out of order or out of balance in your life. I definitely feel there is a message here. You will instinctively know which area of your life your dreams are trying to draw your attention to.

Many of us are fascinated by dreams and their meanings. When I have used my dreams to analyse an aspect of my life it has been, at times, eerily accurate. It's as though a message is trying to get through. I've come to believe that our dreams are, ironically, a way to make us wake up and take notice.

Thinking about your question further, I drew the *Key* card from the *Fortune Reading Cards* by Sharina Star. "This card represents a new way of living opening up to you. It is filled with promises and fresh starts but first you need to let go of the past."

I see the interpretation of your dreams as a key to unlocking an issue from your past. This can pave the way for great healing and clarity. Then you will be truly open for all the wonderful new experiences life has to offer.

Tips on how to decode the dream:

- ♥ Start a dream journal and make notes upon waking when your mind can usually recall the details.
- ♥ Research the meaning of different dreams and see what resonates with you.
- ♥ Be open to the possibility that interpreting your dreams can be a powerful and positive way to improve areas of your life.

Lately, I've had dreams where I'm searching for something. My understanding is this can indicate a loss but maybe it's time I look into that deeper. Now if I could just find my Dream Dictionary…

Today's card has been drawn from the Fortune Reading Cards. All material relating to the card and guidebook is copyright to Sharina Star, 2015.

June 5. 2015

Column 17: As the bard said, be true to yourself

THIS week Sonya asked: "I consider myself to be a positive person so why then is my life not as good as I'd like it to be?"

Just as I was about to return a book to the library, I turned to a page that echoes how I would respond to your question. In her memoir, *Dying to be Me*, Anita Moorjani shares the insights she received from her near-death experience and her miraculous recovery from cancer.

She writes: "When we see someone who's really upbeat, effervescent and kind, but whose life is crumbling, we may think, *See? This 'being positive' thing doesn't work.* But here's the issue: we don't know that individual's inner dialogue. We don't know what other people are telling themselves day in and day out, or whether they're emotionally happy. And most important, we don't know whether they love and value themselves!"

My belief is that our emotional happiness and that inner dialogue hinges upon being true to oneself. But that is only part of the equation. The other part can be summarised by today's Archangel Michael card, *Admit the Truth to Yourself, and Act Accordingly.*

So what is this truth that I'm referring to? It can take many forms: pursuing a career or passion that you love, being creative, being more active, spending quality time with your loved ones….essentially anything that your heart desires. It could be as simple as choosing to not stack the dishwasher out of responsibility but rather to wait for a time during the day when you're in a better head space to do it!

Tips on how to handle the truth:

♥ Our truth gets muffled and overshadowed by our daily activities – stop, breathe and listen to your soul's messages.

♥ If you've noticed an area of your life that is lacking authenticity and integrity, now is the time to make changes – because if not now, when?

♥ Ask: "What am I doing today to create the life I want to experience tomorrow?" Time for truth to be met with action.

Sometimes we sugarcoat, overlook and keep the peace under the guise of being optimistic and positive but in the process we shelve our inner truth. This is deep, I know…and a notion that most people don't give a second thought to as they go about their day. But could it be that ignoring the truth consistently is the cause of why so many people feel like they're just existing, floating and surviving through life?

Don't get me wrong, optimism has its place, but in the words of Shakespeare, "To thine own self be true."

Today's card has been drawn from the Archangel Michael Oracle Cards. All material relating to the card and guidebook is copyright to Doreen Virtue, 2009.

June 12. 2015

Column 18: Be open to unlimited possibilities

THIS week Scott asked: "I don't believe in much, I don't even read my horoscope, so what could your cards possibly tell someone like me?"

Well, any angel or oracle cards and the guidance they represent can tell you quite a lot. The issue is how much of it will permeate your being in this non-believer state that you mention.

Even saying the words that come naturally to me, "I'll tune into your question as I shuffle the cards," would cause you to feel what I refer to as resistance. In other words, it will stir within you more annoyance and irritation than bring a sense of appeasement. Yet I believe today's card, *Possibilities* from the *Osho Zen Tarot,* is the best place to start.

I'll admit that it's not some earth-shattering epiphany-like card, but it is what you're looking for – even if you don't yet believe it!

I have to be honest and say I was relieved that the cards *Letting Go* or *Consciousness* didn't emerge, as that might further drive you away from a world of "possibilities". However the thing about card readings is that they are often a highly accurate measure of what is going on in someone's life and they provide gentle and reassuring guidance…always.

Tips on how to be open to possibilities:

♥ Start with the little things – can you at least bring yourself to appreciate a meal, a sunset, your paycheck?

♥ Ask yourself, "What's the worst that can happen, if just for a while, I make an attempt to look beyond what it is I think I know?"

♥ Consider that life is meant to deliver more to you than the mediocre and that the key to that life is in your hands.

I don't believe you can go from being a non-believer one day to having an unshakable faith the next – at least not without the help of a near-death experience or some major life event (aka a wake-up call).

But don't take my word for it. I refer to a passage that accompanied the *Possibilities* card. "Those who remain content easily remain small: small are their joys, small are their ecstasies, small are their silences, small is their being. But there is no need! This smallness is your own imposition upon your freedom, upon your unlimited possibilities, upon your unlimited potential."

As you go about your life, I hope that you might recall this exchange and at some point recognise that all it takes is to open your eyes even the slightest to be aware of opportunities and your potential. Something may happen that makes your non-believer status a thing of the past and your life will never be the same again. It could be better than you ever imagined.

Today's card has been drawn from the Osho Zen Tarot: The Transcendental Game of Zen. All material relating to the card and guidebook is copyright to Osho International Foundation Switzerland, 1995.

June 19, 2015

Column 19: A reminder to have fun!

THIS week Barbara asked: "I'm sick and tired of the same old, same old. My life is predictable and there's not much excitement. Can the cards shed some light on that?"

This theme is a recurring one because so many feel the same way. I'm going to go out on a limb here and say that what is missing is the F-word. But before you go jumping to conclusions (or writing to the editor), I'm referring to FUN!

Many of us have forgotten what it feels like to have fun. We see glimpses of it, but on a day-to-day basis those fun-filled moments are few and far between. We seem to spend more time gravitating between the serious and the mundane. What's more, we often get so busy that we don't ever stop to consider what it is that makes our heart sing.

So don't worry, you've come to the right place for a healthy injection of fun as the card, *Laughter Is the Best Medicine* from Doreen Virtue's *Archangel Raphael Healing Oracle Cards,* has appeared.

The guidebook which comes with these cards offers some good advice, "…it may be difficult for you to smile right now, but there's always a big release after a good laugh." I've mentioned in a previous column about having a fun makeover, but what could that actually entail?

Tips on how to go from boring to blissful:

♥ Can you see areas of your life where you can detach from the drama? This will help you to relax.
♥ Routines make us feel safe and secure, yet over time they can also diminish our soul's spark. Spontaneity and fun go hand in hand so less planning and more going with the flow.
♥ Reconnect with your inner child. Children are silliness experts – we could do with some of their cheerfulness and amusing behaviours.

It might help to know that Esther and Jerry Hicks, through the Teachings of Abraham, encourage us all to live with this mantra in mind: "The basis of your life: Absolute freedom. The purpose of your life: Joy. The result of your life: Expansion."

To jazz up ordinary moments, putting on a CD or iPod and setting to random can do the trick. Let's just say I now go about my housework with an extra spring (and swing!) in my step. The kids embrace my craziness in these moments – and isn't that the point – because there are no rules when it comes to having fun. Think that scene in *Risky Business* where Tom Cruise's character embraces freedom and fun by dancing to "Old Time Rock and Roll" dressed in nothing but a shirt, socks and jocks.

Other times, just by wearing my sunstone crystal I feel I have a sunnier disposition. Time for you to discover what gives you the most joy and pursue it with pure abandon.

Go ahead, have a good chuckle, chortle or guffaw…and don't give a rats about what others think!

Today's card has been drawn from the Archangel Raphael Healing Oracle Cards. All material relating to the card and guidebook is copyright to Doreen Virtue, 2010.

June 26, 2015

Column 20: Positive thinking powerful

THIS week Liisa asked: "I'm coming down with one illness after another. When will it end, and why me?"

There's a really simple answer to this, but it might be a hard pill to swallow…at least at first.

Within a few hours of receiving your question, a book by Aussie author Craig Harper outlining *30 principles for a better life,* landed on my desk. While it is filled with great anecdotes, the phrase that stood out to me to help answer your question was: "We are both the problem and the solution." Powerful stuff.

There is so much material available about how we create our own reality – it is a cornerstone of modern self-help philosophy. Putting it into practice can seem difficult for us humans. However, it is a big part of why we are here – to master our own destiny. Rather than feeling like we are powerless when it comes to our life experiences (such as being sick), we have to look beyond our self-limiting beliefs about what is possible.

Being constantly ill can feel like a vicious cycle because it can be challenging to feel anything else other than the physical symptoms at the time. It can seem all-consuming. The key is to refocus. It's about switching from feeling negative emotions about the situation to feeling positive emotions, without creating further resistance. There are a number of ways to do this.

Tips on how to go from being encumbered to empowered:

♥ For fast results, stop telling the sickness story. Every time we describe our ailments and illnesses to others, we are sending out a vibrational frequency to bring in more of the same.

♥ Start a positivity journal. When you feel unwell, write down all of the things that feel 'right' in your life. Appreciation has the power to reverse a negative downward spiral.

♥ Know that physical symptoms are your body's way of getting a message to you. Often it is the only way we will listen, take notice and make changes. What is your body trying to tell you? Where can you take better care of yourself? Where can you make changes?

Once again, I deferred to my self-help masters, Esther and Jerry Hicks, through the Teachings of Abraham. Thinking about your question, I shuffled their *Law of Attraction Cards* and received the very appropriately titled card *My Thoughts Are in Harmony with Health.*

You deserve to have good health – we all do. It really comes down to how much you are resisting or allowing good health into your life.

Consider your question as a positive step in the right direction. You have identified the problem, and now you can be part of the solution. If that's not empowering, I don't know what is!

Today's card has been drawn from The Law of Attraction Cards. All material relating to the card and guidebook is copyright to Esther and Jerry Hicks, 2008.

July 3, 2015

Column 21: Embrace your authenticity

THIS week Anne asked: "I have been feeling really anxious lately but have absolutely no reason to feel this way. What's happening to me?"

In the same way that last week's column revealed that our physical symptoms are a way of sending messages to us, so too do our emotions. Your anxiety may be communicating to you an inner restlessness.

While I was preparing my answer, I came across Robin Sharma's book, *Discover Your Destiny With The Monk Who Sold His Ferrari: The 7 Stages of Self-Awakening*. He writes: "This book is dedicated to fellow seekers, those brave souls who exercise the courage to leave the crowd and find their way home to a place called authenticity. May your resolve to awaken and live in *true* power be indomitable…And may you shine so brightly that, at the end of your days, all will pause and say, 'Ah, there was one who lived life fully and completely.'"

Although I would prefer not to answer a question with a question, my response requires me to ask, "Can you say you are living your life fully and completely?"

If the answer is "Yes", then this comes as confirmation – as a "Bravo!" – to your efforts. If however, you paused or answered "No", then now is the time to take stock and consider making changes. Your aim is to align with your "true power".

I wasn't surprised to turn over the *Artistic Expression* card from Doreen Virtue's *Ascended Masters Oracle Cards*. Even if you answered, "Yes" to my previous question, this card comes to emphasise the role of creativity in living a full and complete life.

You don't have to aspire to become the next Picasso (unless of course that resonates with you). It doesn't matter what form the creativity takes. You can be creative cooking, gardening, renovating or as you go about your work. I'm being creative now as the words take shape for this column! And while I think about it, the enjoyment I get from writing illustrates perfectly why we all need something to make us feel alive.

Tips on how to ignite that creative spark:

♥ Is there a passion or creative pursuit that has been dormant within you? In what ways can you free your creativity?
♥ Create more opportunities to create. Grant yourself the time and space to explore your inner artist.
♥ Any time you are feeling creative or inspired to take action, do so. Don't stifle it with restrictions or limits. Rationality and creativity are like oil and water, they do not mix well!

Recently, I rediscovered a friend's artwork. I was so taken by her talent that I could almost feel the exhilaration she must have felt as her masterpiece came to life. I'm sure she'd agree that her art breathes life into her. Now you've just got to ensure you're doing something that breathes life into you.

Today's card has been drawn from the Ascended Masters Oracle Cards. All material relating to the card and guidebook is copyright to Doreen Virtue, 2007.

July 10, 2015

Column 22: Always live in the moment

THIS week Chrissy asked: "This morning I couldn't find my phone. It was in my bed and when I checked it I seemed to have sent a random text to a client on my contact list while I slept. The message made no sense, and I'm feeling really uneasy about this?"

Apart from telling you that you can call on Archangel Chamuel for lost items (he's never once failed to come through for me), I believe today's column will provide the insight and advice that you have been seeking for some time.

Part of the answer lies in a previous column about dreams and how in our slumber state we can receive messages which we can then apply to our waking hours. The other part lies in today's *Focus* card from Denise Linn's *Soul Coaching Oracle Cards*.

Tips to focus on the here and now:

♥ Awareness is the key. When you find yourself thinking about the wouldas, couldas, shouldas, you're out of the moment. Once you know this, you can just as easily snap back into the present and refocus on what you were doing.

♥ When you're experiencing any big negative emotions such as anger, guilt, criticism or judgement, consider whether it is because you are out of the moment? Most of these feelings by default, draw our attention away from the present by causing us to stew on the past or worry about the future.

♥ Practise mindfulness and live life according to this saying attributed to Bil Keane: "Yesterday's the past, tomorrow's the future, but today is a gift. That's why it's called the present."

Sometimes things happen, like the experience you described, because it prompts us to ask questions. It takes us on a path of self-discovery and as the saying goes, "When the student is ready, the teacher will appear." In your case, I feel you would gain a raft of benefits from exploring the theory and practice of living in the now.

It would be remiss of me to write about the present moment without quoting who I consider to be The Master of The Now (and possibly your new teacher) Eckhart Tolle. In 2011, he was listed as the most spiritually influential person in the world. In other words, he knows a thing or two about living a life with purpose and presence.

Interestingly, I was treated to a serendipity moment when I looked up Eckhart's website and found that he is currently promoting a feature called *Sleep: Merging with the Source of Life.* This serves to confirm that today's column can represent a new path of learning for you. Your energy will go from diffused to determined. Not only will losing your phone be a thing of the past, but you will only be contacting your clients when you are wide awake.

Today's card has been drawn from the Soul Coaching Oracle Cards: What Your Soul Wants You to Know. All material relating to the card and guidebook is copyright to Denise Linn, 2006.

July 17, 2015

Column 23 (part one): Parenthood a constant juggling act

THIS week Maria asked: "I work a lot then when I'm at home I'm busy doing all the other stuff that has to get done. I worry that my kids are missing out?"

This is such a big subject that I'll be answering your question over two weeks.

I started writing a blog once titled: "How much is enough time with your children?" I never got to finish it because the kids were constantly interrupting. The irony is not lost on me. So it seemed fitting to dig out my partial notes to help answer a question that is on the lips of many multitasking parents.

There is no right or wrong answer here and it will be different for each person. I can only say that you will know in your heart what feels like "enough". Are there ways that expenses can be cut or savings made so that you can reduce your working hours? Will it help you to feel more balanced? That is the key.

Striking a delicate balance between structure and spontaneity comes to mind but how can we have both? The point is we *can* have both and both are necessary. It's a matter of tuning into our intuition to know when one ends and the other begins. Also, we need to act on that intuition without delay. When we start doubting, second-guessing or over-analysing what our intuition has guided us to do, we automatically dilute the power behind it.

It might be time for you to become acquainted with the

teachings of Kuan Yin as represented by today's *Compassion* card courtesy of Doreen Virtue.

Tips to clear a path for compassion:

♥ Consider that you're not giving yourself enough credit for the time you *do* spend with your children. Maybe it's a case of quality not quantity.

♥ Acknowledge the contribution you are making. This is not an ego boost but serves as an act of self-appreciation. It also prevents us from looking for appreciation from others.

♥ Know that you are making a difference in the lives of your children, whatever you do.

Like many mothers what you are feeling is something Ita Buttrose referred to in her book *Motherguilt* as, you guessed it, Motherguilt. She writes: "Being a mother is, and always will be, a full-time job…But the strain and responsibility of caring for children plus holding down a job does not allow mothers much time for the joy of parenting."

While this may be true, a close friend once shared some words that gave me a new perspective on motherhood and all of the "stuff" we do for our children. It was along the lines of: "Never take for granted all those things you do 'just because' – every meal, every tuck-in, every wiped tear – it's all love."

Start by having more compassion for yourself and your situation. I'm sure you will conclude that you are doing your best and that's all anyone, including your kids, can ask for.

Today's card has been drawn from the Goddess Guidance Oracle Cards. All material relating to the card and guidebook is copyright to Doreen Virtue, 2004.

Column 23 (part two): Ask Sharon — Let it go

LAST week Maria asked: "I work a lot then when I'm at home I'm busy doing all the other stuff that has to get done. I worry that my kids are missing out?"

For part two of this mammoth question, I shuffled the cards from a different deck to last week and amazingly received the same Ascended Master Quan Yin! Except instead of *Compassion*, the card was *Let It Go*, which again helps guide the advice on this important issue for parents and particularly mums.

I was discussing this subject with another mother recently and my feeling was that our kids are not likely to reminisce and say, "I wish mum had cleaned the floor more" but they might say, "I wish she'd got down on the floor and played with me more!"

This is not about compounding any feelings of guilt, but rather to give you a sense of perspective about the "other stuff". I've resigned to the fact that while my kids are young, these will not be the years I can claim the cleanest house. I do the bare minimum…the wannabe supermum in me died long ago! So today's column is about making peace with where you are in your life and seeing where you can release the unimportant to make room for the things that matter. It's also about keeping in mind what constitutes love and how to achieve balance at the same time.

Tips on how to loosen the reins and let go:

- ♥ Let go of the common misperception that you are meant to feel guilty when you are not with your children. It's ok to enjoy your work and time-out.
- ♥ Let go of your own pre-children standards and expectations, they no longer apply and will only be the source of undue stress and frustration.
- ♥ Let go of the housework, chores and anything that can wait until another day.

There's a poster that sums up that last point: "Good mums have sticky floors, messy kitchens, laundry piles, dirty ovens and happy kids." And just in case I still haven't hit home, I went back to Ita Buttrose's *Motherguilt*. She writes: "Sometimes in their haste to get through all of the things they have to do, working mothers forget some of the most important things in life – like living, for instance. Society not only puts a lot of pressure on working mums, but women put unrealistic pressures on themselves as well. Mothers do not have to be perfect, good enough will do."

My new philosophy in achieving something that resembles a work-life balance goes beyond domesticity. I've stopped being so quick to clip my own wings when it comes to the parenting department. Instead I now recognise, like all well-meaning parents, that what we are aiming to do is give children their own wings so they can fly.

Today's card has been drawn from the Ascended Masters Oracle Cards. All material relating to the card and guidebook is copyright to Doreen Virtue, 2007.

July 31. 2015

Column 24: Sharon says listen to your wise voice

THIS week Jane asked: "I'm not unwell but I'm living in a fog, going from one thing to the next. How can I shake this fuzzy feeling?"

One could be easily mistaken for thinking this week's column would be all about seeing more clearly, yet it was the *Listening* card that appeared from Cheryl Richardson's *Self-Care Cards* to offer you clarity. While this card's message is to, "Listen to your wise self [and] let your inner compass direct the course of your life", I felt there was much more to it than just being guided by your inner voice.

When I was growing up the phrase, "They could talk underwater with a mouthful of marbles" was thrown around a lot...usually in my direction! I admit it, I like to talk...a lot (my husband would certainly vouch for this). Maybe it was originally an attention-seeking thing, maybe it was an immaturity thing, but regardless it took me a while to learn that an important part of communication is to listen to others. It took me even longer to learn to listen to my "wise inner self".

I feel that you are at a place in your life where your next course of action is to listen. Listen and be guided by your instincts without the second-guessing and without the seeking of opinions from others. This is about you and your valid inner nudges. I'll bet you've tried everything else and that explains the fuzziness that has probably become all-too familiar to you.

Another familiar habit that doesn't serve us well is in the way we communicate. How often do you find yourself in a conversation with someone and you are already thinking about what you are going to say next without really listening? We all do it. But we are also missing out on being present, being engaged and being exposed to relevant information that might be the very thing to clear our path.

Signs can come in all forms including things that other people say. Often, many of my serendipity moments come via a statement made by someone else. Why does this synchronicity even matter? Because not only does it feel exhilarating when that moment happens, but it confirms loud and clear that I am on the right path.

Tips on how to create leverage from your listening skills:

- ♥ Be ready to notice when you need to listen to others, listen to your body or listen to your heart.
- ♥ Know that it takes real presence to listen intently to someone else. Yet, the aliveness and richness of your personal interactions will be forever altered for the better.
- ♥ Be aware that the big pay-off from listening to your inner self is the inspiration that always ensues.

It is these moments of inspiration that will guide you out of the fog.

Today's card has been drawn from the Self-Care Cards. All material relating to the card and guidebook is copyright to Cheryl Richardson, 2001.

August 7, 2015

Column 25: We must embrace change

THIS week a question was submitted anonymously: "I get to Monday ready to change my diet but by Tuesday I've lost my motivation and it all seems too hard. How do I stop this vicious cycle?"

I'm going to do something a bit radical. I'm going to address your question about diet without actually referring to food or exercise. WHHAAATT?

The answer to your question revolves around this week's card *Transformation*, from Denise Linn's *Soul Coaching Oracle Cards*.

German Philosopher Friedrich Nietzsche brought our attention to the process of change by saying: "The snake which cannot cast its skin has to die." I'm not suggesting that if you don't make changes in your life you will die, but do you feel like a little piece of you dies inside every time you say you'll do something and you don't carry through?

Consider…the phoenix that rises from the ashes, the lotus that emerges from the mud and the chrysalis that turns into the butterfly. Enough with the transformation metaphors, the point is when you decide you've gone through enough suffering and dissatisfaction, change can be a heartbeat away.

I recently encountered an issue where I realised I was blocking my own potential. The self-sabotaging was frustrating and relentless. It wasn't until I got to the point where I said to myself, "That's enough, time to do something different" that things changed for me. In that instant, I recalled a quote attributed to Einstein and often used by Dr Phil: "The definition of insanity is doing the same thing over and over again and expecting different results." True that!

Change itself is not the enemy; it's our attitude towards it that gives us grief. Sometimes we get carried away with possible outcomes and fears that might never eventuate. Embracing change can be a tough gig. It can be challenging to visualise a different life to the one you keep perpetuating week after week.

Tips on how to eliminate change as the enemy and make peace with it:

- ♥ Momentum – do you treat it like friend or foe? Harness the power of momentum and make it work for you. It's always that first step that is the hardest. Get going and keep going.
- ♥ Size-up your inhibitors to change and cut them off at the pass. Are you afraid of what others will think (or say), of failure, or of your own power and potential?
- ♥ Remember, it's not about wanting to throw the towel in on change, it's about not giving up on yourself.

We all seek change in some way, and it's just as well because like death and taxes it's one thing we can't escape. Inherently we know that change will lead to a bigger, better, brighter life…the one we came here to live.

Today's card has been drawn from the Soul Coaching Oracle Cards: What Your Soul Wants You to Know. All material relating to the card and guidebook is copyright to Denise Linn, 2006.

August 14, 2015

Column 26: Our dreams have meaning

THIS week Lou asked: "I have a recurring dream in which I'm terrified to fly. I actually love air travel. What's going on with that?"

In a previous column featuring dreams I acknowledged that I'm no dream expert. For me it's about interpreting information…in the same way that I interpret the cards.

So let's get interpreting to un-taint your love of air travel. Pick up any dream book or click on any dream website and you will see flying features quite prominently. This might help you to feel as though you're not alone in the "terrified to fly" while dreaming department.

A dream in which you're flying is often about freedom and letting go. One could deduce then, that if you're afraid of flying in your dream that there could be something that you're afraid to let go of or something that is inhibiting your sense of freedom. Trust your instincts on this one – usually the first thing that comes to mind (or whatever stirs up the most emotions) is it.

The next piece of information to help you unravel your flying mystery is today's card, *You're Ready* from Doreen Virtue's *Angel Answers Oracle Cards*.

With that sense of eagerness, I looked deeper into your dream question and came across Sigmund Freud who argued that flying represented dreams of a sexual nature. But I think that's a whole other column! For today we'll keep it PG and stick to letting go and finding freedom.

So I found a safe haven in Rose Inserra's *Dictionary of Dreams*. "Dreams can help us understand ourselves better. If we interpret them correctly, we can find a treasure trove of hidden secrets. Who or what are we running away from in a chase scenario? If our teeth are falling out, should we be paying the dentist a visit or is it all to do with losing our grip on things?"

Tips on how to unlock and unravel the message of your dreams:

♥ First, acknowledge that your dreams do serve a purpose other than to aid sleep. If you dismiss them as such, you won't be open to their "hidden secrets".

♥ Can you make links between your recurring dreams and any past issues that require reconciling?

♥ Look at this as an opportunity to learn something about yourself as opposed to highlighting a problem. There's no need for judgement when you're decoding dreams.

For many, there is something beneath the surface (a childhood issue, a trauma, a fear) that can be the very thing that is blocking their path to happiness. Dreams are a way that we receive messages about these issues that need to be cleared. When you identify what it is for you and heal that issue, the dream will no longer persist. Instead, it will allow your real dreams to take flight.

Today's card has been drawn from the Angel Answers Oracle Cards. All material relating to the card and guidebook is copyright to Doreen Virtue and Radleigh Valentine, 2014.

August 21. 2015

Column 27: Don't rush your recovery

THIS week Carla asked: "Just about everyone I know has been sick including myself. I am feeling better, but I still can't be bothered getting out and about. What can I do?"

It's interesting that we defer to the "What can I do?" question when really what we need to ask is, "How can I be?" So much of what we "do" comes from believing that our logic shapes our lives. It gives us a sense of control. When it comes to our health and we get sick, or those around us are sick, we lose control over the situation. No amount of pills or potions can overcome that feeling of helplessness.

Often, when we have just a hint of feeling better, we jump straight back into where we left off. Intellectually, this is a good plan of action, but only once we have fully recovered. Our mind convinces us that we don't have the time to ease back into life. So I would encourage you to look at your state of demotivation as a sign to take a bit longer to recover.

The *Door to Spirit* card from Sandra Anne Taylor's *Energy Oracle Cards* signals that this is a good time to connect with your higher self. When nothing else gets you through, it is always available. It is infallible. Trust it like a good friend on hand at a moment's notice. And you don't have to sit cross-legged, yogi-style to appreciate what your Spirit is trying to tell you!

In *The Power of Your Spirit*, bestselling author Sonia Choquette writes: "Connecting with Spirit is the most authentic, lasting power we have in our lives. We can't control the outside world, but with the power of Spirit, we can create a sense of purpose within that brings about deep satisfaction and personal peace – regardless of what is going on around us."

Tips on how to connect with Spirit and let it carry us through life's challenges:

♥   The daily grind is a constant noise and distraction to our inner self. The key is to get still and quiet enough to hear those messages that can lead you away from the dark and into the light.

♥   Where can you commit a few moments out of your day to go within? This is not a time for list-making, planning or analysing.

♥   Swap resilience for rejuvenation and in the process discover what it feels like to be guided by Spirit instead of the space between our ears.

At first it can be hard to believe such a basic practice can help at all, which is why many don't begin it in the first place. But what have you got to lose, except a few minutes of worry and stress in place of a few minutes of peace and calm? That's enough of an incentive for me to give it a try…how about you?

Today's card has been drawn from the Energy Oracle Cards. All material relating to the card and guidebook is copyright to Sandra Anne Taylor, 2013.

August 28, 2015

Column 28: Remember the big picture

THIS week Liz asked: "The years are passing by so quickly and I never get to do the things that really matter to me. What can I do about it?"

There's the list of things that we need to do daily, then deep in the recess of our mind is our 'wish list'. These are the things that if we had more time, money and energy we would jump at. And because they are not considered priorities, they remain as wishes – desires that go unfulfilled.

The problem is that these desires don't go away. When something is important and you continue to ignore it, there is a constant feeling of dissatisfaction. For many, it is the daily grind that takes precedence over more meaningful activities and as a result one's level of fulfillment is affected.

In *Take Time for Your Life*, bestselling author and life coach, Cheryl Richardson, encourages us to: "Imagine for a moment that cords of energy run from your body to everything undone or incomplete in your life. Some cords are wider than others, representing those items that have more energy flowing to them (often the items that we fear the most, like the unfiled tax returns or the medical problem we've been avoiding)."

This week's card, *Focus* from Colette Baron-Reid's *The Wisdom of Avalon Oracle Cards*, depicts a path leading into a forest. Most are familiar with the phrase, "Can't see the forest for the trees", where we are so engrossed in the details that we fail to see the bigger picture. And that is really what the answer to your question is about.

Tips on how to back yourself and not back out of what really matters:

- ♥ Be mindful of how often you have inspirational ideas or projects but then quash them with 'logical' reasons not to carry through.
- ♥ Don't underestimate the feeling of accomplishment. When we set out to achieve something and take the steps toward it, the sense of triumph can bring tremendous joy.
- ♥ Write down your wish list and pick one thing to "focus" on. Sometimes we have so many things we'd like to do that we decide not to pursue anything – so choose just one and commit to that.

My "one thing" to focus on has been exercise, more accurately to get outdoors in the sunshine and walk. I saw a TV advertisement about Steptember and took this as my sign. The fact that you get to exercise and help people with cerebral palsy only adds to the good feeling of doing something that matters.

For added motivation, I used my Flybuys points for the latest and greatest fitness-gadget, a Fitbit. I've charged my iPod and donned my sneakers, now if I could just find my Nike shirt…

Today's card has been drawn from The Wisdom of Avalon Oracle Cards. All material relating to the card and guidebook is copyright to Colette Baron-Reid, 2007.

♥ *Colette Baron-Reid commented on this post on Facebook by saying, "COOL!!!!"*

September 4, 2015

SPECIAL EDITION for Father's Day (part one): Take time to show your dad you care

IN my Mother's Day column, I encouraged those in any mother's inner circle to deliver something important to mums to honour that holiday. I wasn't talking about gifts. Now the time has come to consider another significant relationship and all things fatherhood so that we may honour, cherish and celebrate dads everywhere.

It is interesting that both Mother's and Father's Day began out of the mourning of the loss of a parent. Anna Jarvis' celebration of her mother after she died inspired what we now know as Mother's Day. Once again I consulted Wikipedia to discover that Grace Golden Clayton was grieving the loss of her father in 1907. He was one of 362 men, of which 250 were fathers, killed in the Monongah Mining Disaster. This tragedy resulted in around 1,000 children without dads.

It wouldn't be until 1966 that Father's Day became official in the U.S. Despite its late start, it was only a matter of time until the rest of the world caught on to the importance of applauding fathers.

So what is it that dads would like from us this Sunday to show we care? While I'm risking receiving hate mail from local hardware stores, you might be surprised to know that it's not more tools! Let me clarify – tools are only as good as the time dads get to use them – and this is where we can help.

Tips on how to show dad that he IS the sharpest tool in the shed:

♥ Find out what dad's currency is. It might be some time with mates or time in the garden. Help make it happen and you're guaranteed a happy dad.
♥ Let dad know that everything he does for the family is appreciated…and that you love him even when he has a grumpy moment.
♥ Support his dreams. In Buddhism this is referred to as sympathetic joy. We covered it for Mother's Day and now it's time to help dad discover what's on his bucket list.

I'm not into pandering, placating or pussyfooting but I am all about health, harmony and happiness, so in the interest of the latter three, I would encourage you take the time this Father's Day to really get to know dad.

I sense the difference in my husband if he comes home from work to a harmonious environment. This is not about invalidating the mum's day as she hands the kids to dad quicker than you can say, "What's for dinner?" It's just that many dads make a direct link to what they're doing 'out there' to support the family with the degree of happiness in the home.

Next week I'll be looking more deeply into the importance of fathers and how we can celebrate them beyond this Sunday.

September 11, 2015

SPECIAL EDITION for Father's Day (part two): Cherish precious moments

LAST week I considered the origins of Father's Day and how we can consistently show dads that we really care. Just like the issues that emerged while I prepared the Mother's Day column, it became clearer that how we treat our parents, and in this case our dads, is a big deal.

This week it's about looking at how the role of fatherhood has changed. While contemplating the issues of fatherhood, and reflecting on my own experiences, I found myself asking the question: "Is it just that over time, we have come to expect more of dads or is it because everybody – men, women and even some children – are so busy that we have become more demanding of ourselves, and others?"

I immediately recalled a moment from an episode of Dr Phil. He was covering a show on relationships and specifically the role of the man in the family. Dr Phil said it best: "If men want to be successful in their marriage and family life, they have to change and broaden their definition of what it means to be successful as a man. Being a good provider, protector, leader and teacher is a privilege that comes with responsibilities that many men aren't aware of."

For some time we have been looking to dads as more than the traditional financial providers, but has anyone actually bothered to discuss these extra demands with them? It seems that we, as a society, expect dads to just step up and own this new role. Somewhere along the way, have we expected *him* to know and embrace these added responsibilities – this new way of being *the rock* of the family unit?

Tips on how to be "the rock" of the family and not let it weigh you down:

♥ If your childhood was difficult, don't use it as a filter. You are your own person with your own style of parenting.

♥ Never underestimate the value of quality time with your kids (or grandkids) and let it bring out the kid at heart.

♥ Post Father's Day, whenever you can, loosen the reins on responsibilities and rules and have some fun!

This week raised more questions than answers around the subject of fatherhood.

To seek extra clarity, I thought why not look to "The Rock" himself and get his take on it. Despite a busy Hollywood schedule, Dwayne The Rock Johnson has claimed that even on the road, he finds the time to call his partner and daughter every day. While it's not the usual parenting situation (and really, what is?), this demonstrates that connecting with our family and showing our love is still, and always will be, most important.

September 18, 2015

Column 29: Take time to reach out to loved ones

THIS week Jen asked: "My sister and I are not as close as when we were kids. Is it because we live apart or because we have issues we've never talked about?"

It seems to be a natural part of the rhythm of life that people drift in and out. For most, it's not a problem and there's an acceptance that not everyone who comes into one's life is meant to be there until the very end...including some family members.

But there is something about family – whether blood-related or not – that implies a lasting connection.

Often life can get in the way of having more enriching relationships. Even reflecting on the origins of the relationship and how it once bloomed, may cause us to feel sorrow because that is no longer our experience. It has become a memory, not the present reality that we had hoped for. However, this reminiscing can also be the spark we need to reignite that connection.

Today the *why* is not as relevant as the *what you do now*. Denise Linn's *Mending Bridges* card comes to you, and anyone else, who is need of relationship repair.

Tips on how to extend the olive branch and still honour your feelings:

♥ Reconnection has power. You are more likely to feel peace and closure in the attempt at reaching out to a long-lost loved one, regardless of the outcome.

71

♥ Keep the interaction in the present. Don't let the past overshadow the potential for healing.

♥ Consider, if you knew how much time you had left to live, who would you reach out to? Is the fear of being hurt stopping you, and can you find the courage to overcome it?

Sometimes a situation requires someone to be the hero (or in your case the heroine). For a stalemate to be lifted, someone inevitably needs to step up and reach out to the other without fear of consequences. This detachment to the outcome paves the way for possibilities...and healing for all concerned. It is unconditional love in action.

With the September 11 anniversary fresh in my mind, I was reminded of Robert Holden's book *Success Intelligence*, where he recalls that day, and the phone calls made by the passengers aboard the three aeroplanes.

He points out that all the calls were made to loved ones. He cuts to the heart of the issue by saying: "All of these passengers would be dead in just a few moments. Their last act was to do what is important – they made their phone calls, they declared their love. These passengers were teaching us all that in the final call, love is the goal, love is the reason and love is the whole point of everything."

Today's card has been drawn from the Gateway Oracle Cards. All material relating to the card and guidebook is copyright to Denise Linn, 2012.

♥ *Denise Linn liked this post on Facebook.*

Column 30: Declutter for superior sleep

THIS week Melissa asked: "Have you got any tips on how to get a good night's sleep?"

When I drew Denise Linn's *Renewing Your Life* card depicting a person pushing a box of clutter off a cliff, I knew how this could help you.

Recently I've embarked on my own possession purging process, only to then make the link between clutter and restless sleep.

Most articles written about getting a better night's sleep focus on some common hints such as: Have a regular bedtime and wake up time (something to do with circadian rhythms), and stop all stimulants like coffee and chocolate close to bedtime. But when you've put these suggestions into practice and you're still not sleeping well, what then?

While I'm not a chronic insomniac, I've had plenty of nights spent lying awake trying to get to sleep or back to sleep. I put it down to poor sleeping habits developed over many years. I'd like to blame it on my days of university partying, but it was established long before that.

Before I engaged in some fierce decluttering, I enlisted help. Thankfully, my husband was happy to spend quality time with the kids, and having my mum's assistance was a huge advantage (multitasking as the voice of reason and chief tea-maker).

As I picked up each item, I asked myself, "Do I love it, do I use it?" which soon helped me sort my stuff. I let one thing lead me to another, and while at times my bedroom looked like a small bomb had detonated, there was soon order amongst the chaos. What I discovered is that when I uncluttered my bedroom, my sleep immediately improved.

Tips on how to clear your clutter for superior sleep:

♥ Accept that there will be moments where you feel overwhelmed and you're surrounded by more mess than when you started.

♥ Questions about your own level of materialism may surface. This can be as much an emotional experience as it is a physical one.

♥ Throughout this process consider this, as paraphrased from the great book itself, "We come into this life with nothing and we'll leave with nothing."

♥ Be prepared to make tough decisions about your "stuff" but don't let it stall your efforts.

As I blasted through box after box and item after item, I found myself summoning a new energy and vitality. It made me forget that the night before I'd had one of my very ordinary night's sleeps! I really did start to feel like I'd "renewed" my life and myself. When you keep your eye on the prize of how good you'll feel after your space clearing, you won't look back.

During my decluttering I stumbled upon a reference to Chuck Palahniuk's novel, *Fight Club,* which is based on the central character's struggle with insomnia and consumerism. How apt to read that, "The things you used to own, now they own you." Touché!

Today's card has been drawn from the Gateway Oracle Cards. All material relating to the card and guidebook is copyright to Denise Linn, 2012.

October 2, 2015

Column 31: You don't have to follow along

THIS week a question was submitted anonymously: "I went to a family BBQ and I realised I'm not like them anymore, it was confronting to see the way they carried on. I love my family but what does all this mean?"

When we get together with family it's usually a happy affair, but occasionally it makes us reflect on the past and reassess our own life. It can cast a spotlight on where we've been, where we are and where we're going. This is what can feel so "confronting".

The *Osho Zen Tarot* card *Conditioning* explains a lot. "This card recalls an old Zen story, about a lion who was brought up by sheep and who thought he was a sheep until an old lion captured him and took him to a pond, where he showed him his own reflection. Many of us are like this lion – the image we have of ourselves comes not from our own direct experience but from the opinions of others."

What you are discovering on your path of self-improvement is how to be a lion (or lioness), not a sheep. Maybe you want more from your life, and that's ok. Maybe the other members of your family are content to stay where they are, and that's ok too.

Tips on how to let your individuality shine without it dimming those around you:

- ♥ See your epiphany as a breakthrough and that this is the time to break out of the mould.
- ♥ Let any judgement of others pass by as quickly as it enters your awareness. That judgement will only hold you back.
- ♥ Don't deny your feelings. You have every right to be the person you were destined to be.

You can be an individual and still love your family. However, when a person experiences personal growth, it can make others around them question their direction (or lack of). Still, this is not your concern. It's one of the hardest truths to face when being true to yourself – that you have no control over another's reactions. So you have to remain courageous in your convictions. It's a case of each to their own journey.

When you know with confidence that you are ready for change, that you are excited by the possibilities and nothing can stand in your way, you can actually inspire others to do the same. You can effect change by remaining steadfast on your path. The key is to not do it for that purpose. Do it for yourself – if your family comes along with you, that's a bonus.

Next time you feel crowded by your family (or anyone else for that matter), just remember you are always free to choose to NOT follow the crowd.

Today's card has been drawn from the Osho Zen Tarot: The Transcendental Game of Zen. All material relating to the card and guidebook is copyright to Osho International Foundation Switzerland, 1995.

October 9, 2015

Column 32: Loved ones want to help

THIS week Doreen asks: "At 82, I limit myself to driving short trips so my daughter has to take me to appointments etc. I'm struggling with having to rely on others. What do you suggest?"

I'm sure your daughter would admit that she is only too happy to take you places. She might even say it's the least she can do after all the things you've done for her. But I suspect that doesn't make you feel any better.

Cheryl Richardson's *Help* card conveys it best: "Ask for help. Receiving is an act of generosity." Many don't see help in this way (even when offered by family members), and are uncomfortable with it, as you have alluded to.

Today's card means that we are being generous of spirit when we receive because to do otherwise is to deny someone else the feeling they get from giving.

We all know that warm and fuzzy feeling we get when we help another in need. Being of service is an admirable quality. So why then when someone reaches out to us or offers to help, our natural instinct is often to refuse?

Probably the number one reason we decline help is because we don't want to be a burden to others or inconvenience them. I suspect this is exacerbated as we age. This is where trust is required. We have to learn to trust that if someone has offered to do something for us that they have thought it through and wouldn't be offering otherwise. A simple "thank you" will do.

It takes practice to accept help in this way, despite the

simplicity of such a gesture. This can be especially hard for people who have given a lot of themselves and are not familiar with accepting help.

Tips on how to reframe our rationale on receiving:

- ♥ When someone makes an offer, say "yes" and trust that it has come to you for a reason. Treat it like the gift that it is.
- ♥ Visualise a set of scales next time you're trying to decide whether you're out of balance in the giving and receiving departments.
- ♥ Instead of thinking that you rely on others, consider that you are allowing others to help, which in turn makes them feel good.

It might feel like we've come full circle, but see if you can elevate your feeling of frustration to one of mutual love and affection. Keep in mind that what your daughter is doing is showing you that she loves and cares for you. It's not about pity or obligation, but pure unconditional love.

If all else fails, there's that Beatles song that would be worth listening to in the car with your daughter to lighten the situation. *"When I was younger so much younger than today…"*

Today's card has been drawn from the Self-Care Cards. All material relating to the card and guidebook is copyright to Cheryl Richardson, 2001.

> ♥ *Cheryl Richardson liked this post on Facebook by putting three hearts in the comments.*

October 16, 2015

Column 33 (part one): True love can be magical

THIS week Maggie asks: "I've been divorced for a while and it's difficult to meet new people. How can I find a partner to share my life with?"

Love...there have been songs and sonnets written about it, but how do we truly open our heart?

Most people don't realise that at their core – their essence – is love. So when we experience love with another, it's as though you have plugged into that energy. It helps you to recall who you really are. And that's why it feels so darn good!

Relationship guru and bestselling author of *Men Are from Mars, Women Are from Venus*, Dr John Gray, gets to the heart of the issue. He writes: "Many times, people are looking for their partner and they say they can't find them. Well, if your soul mate is not knocking on your door, it's because you're not ready. If you want to find someone who can fully love you and know you, you have to know and love yourself."

Denise Linn's card *Opening to Love* reiterates this truth, so now you have a very clear task at hand. You might feel that you've already been opening your heart to love and that you've had plenty of time on your own, but now it's about going deeper.

Most of us find it easy to love the people around us, but it's the loving ourselves part that can trip us up. Could it be that we can't see past the concept as being airy-fairy or that we don't really know what it entails? Regardless of the reason it doesn't make it any less important.

Tips on how to become acquainted with loving yourself before becoming acquainted with another:

♥ If you're feeling a lack of confidence, try the "fake it until you make it" approach. Even Wikihow says that emotions can take a bit of time to catch up with behaviours.

♥ Surrender timing and expectations. These are the biggest blocks because it places your focus on what's *not* happening, rather than being positive about what *is*.

♥ Following your bliss is another great strategy. In the very least, you'll be having fun until your soul mate knocks at your door!

I'm not trying to downplay that having a companion is important to you, but if you can believe that you are perfect, whole and complete just as you are, then you are on the fast track to relationship bliss. Make this your new attitude and your biggest problem may then be having so many possible partners to choose from that you'll be beating them back with a stick!

This topic is a biggie, so I'll be exploring it further next week.

Today's card has been drawn from the Gateway Oracle Cards. All material relating to the card and guidebook is copyright to Denise Linn, 2012.

♥ *Dr John Gray liked this post on Facebook.*

October 23, 2015

Column 33 (part two): Self-love the key to true happiness

LAST week Maggie asked: "I've been divorced for a while and it's difficult to meet new people. How can I find a partner to share my life with?"

The gist of my response was that if you take care of your relationship with yourself, your relationships with others will take care of themselves.

For part two of this epic topic, consider yourself enrolled in Self-Love 101.

Self-love is the linchpin of all self-help philosophy. The key is putting it into practice. If you do, you can attain not only harmonious relationships, but good health, prosperity and generally a happy life.

Self-approval and self-acceptance go hand in hand with self-love. If we do things for approval from others, we are only setting ourselves up for heartache. At a whim our self-esteem and moods can be affected by what is going on around us. Constantly reacting to things people say or do, or circumstances, is futile.

A pre-requisite of loving the self is identifying what makes you happy…but anything external will only provide a short-term burst of fulfillment. So it's about finding out what makes your heart sing. Outside influences have no bearing. Has it been a while since you asked yourself, "What makes me happy?"

Tips on how to get your daily dose of self-love:

♥ Nurture yourself (eating healthily, exercising, taking time-out).

♥ Speak kindly to yourself ensuring that your inner dialogue is always positive.

♥ Try not to overcommit – don't say "yes" when you really mean "no".

That inner dialogue in particular is worth paying attention to. It's an indication of whether we're engaging in self-love or not. Is it kind, loving and empowering or berating, judgmental and full of "shoulds"?

It would be remiss of me to write about this topic without deferring to the one who made self-love available to the masses. The central theme of Louise Hay's *You Can Heal Your Life* is loving the self by changing the way you think. It has sold over 40 million copies…now that's a lot of loving!

The message is that if you can learn to love yourself – regardless of the experiences you've had – you can change your life for the better. Louise declares that: "Life is really very simple. What we give out, we get back. What we think about ourselves becomes the truth for us."

For some this can be frightening, for others liberating. But it makes sense to harness that power to create the reality that we truly desire.

While writing this, I made myself a cup of my favourite tea coincidentally called "Love". It just goes to show that it can be the little things we do for ourselves that really make the difference.

October 30, 2015

Column 34 (Halloween Special): Release the skeletons in the closet

THIS week Charlene asked: "I want to start a new business but how can I clear obstacles and blocks I've been experiencing?"

Sometimes as we approach certain milestones, ghosts of the past pay us a visit. They can present themselves as those "obstacles and blocks" that you refer to.

When we encounter these obstructions, it's our tendency to want to remove them as quickly as they appear. Yet to deny that they serve a purpose is to do yourself an injustice.

If you haven't yet achieved your desired outcome, it's because people and situations are still in the process of lining up. It's about timing and allowing things to unfold to get you the best possible results. It's also about trust on all levels.

This is not all doom and gloom. As I drew the *You Can Do It* card represented by Archangel Michael, the energy around it was very strong, positive and determined. You can take these same qualities into your venture.

While my advice has been centred on trusting the process of life, this card has come to give you the surety that it is a case of *when* your business will happen not *if*.

In the meantime, the road ahead can be less bumpy for you. See that this current imposition is actually an opportunity to put into practice the talents, skills and wisdom from your accumulated life experiences.

Tips on how to release the skeletons in your closet and not let them rattle you:

♥ Trust your instinct to know exactly what your blockages are. Sometimes identifying them alone can bring relief.

♥ Like the boogeyman, are the challenges you're facing real or projections of what *might* happen? Letting go of the surmising, speculating and overanalysing will help here.

♥ Acknowledge that once the lesson has been learned from this experience you can move on. Your energy and enthusiasm can be better utilised working toward your goal.

When you are on the precipice of something new, it's natural to feel scared. Interestingly, some people are as afraid of success as they are of failure! Either way, it's time to come out of the shadows. Terror can be tamed.

You know a book is good when the title has been trademarked. *Feel the Fear and Do It Anyway* has become a common expression for good reason. Author, Susan Jeffers, pointed out that: "Underlying all our fears is a lack of trust in ourselves." So if you can learn to trust and back yourself, these obstacles and blocks will be no more. And just maybe you can do as so many others will be doing this Halloween and turn fear into fun.

Today's card has been drawn from the Ascended Masters Oracle Cards. All material relating to the card and guidebook is copyright to Doreen Virtue, 2007.

November 6, 2015

Column 35: Don't overcommit yourself

THIS week Jeanette asked: "I want to help people but then I overcommit myself and feel overwhelmed. How do I make it better?"

Your topic begs the question, "Is all help good help?" In order to take our responsibilities seriously but not to the point of burnout, it's important to know your physical limits – we all have them.

Reading my son's school newsletter recently, I came across the section on virtues. Responsibility was being featured. It was about being dependable, keeping agreements and giving your best. If you've made a commitment to help and afterwards you feel pressure and overextended, then regardless of your good intentions, you cannot possibly give your best. And as you're discovering, this is also not good for you. The thing about being overcommitted is it not only affects your performance but it affects your health, moods, and you can forget about any level of inner peace!

Tips on how to help without hitting the wall:

♥ Make discernment your new best friend. Selecting meaningful activities that are congruent with you and your lifestyle are paramount.

♥ Before you take a new task to task, pause before you reply. There is no harm in saying, "I'll think it over", before you commit.

♥ Redefine the to-do list and release the pressure valve by keeping it lighthearted. Meeting responsibilities might be serious business, but your attitude toward them doesn't have to be.

Marianne Williamson's *Personal Power* card comes as a reminder that, "Achievement doesn't come from what we do, but from who we are. Our worldly power results from our personal power."

While writing this, my five-year-old son handed me a book from our shelf titled, *Meditations for Women Who Do Too Much* by Anne Wilson Schaef. He didn't know that I was in the process of seeking a quote for my next column...not to mention he's still learning to read!

While this little book is full of wisdom and advice, I couldn't go past the Introduction to emphasise my point. Thanks to my son's intuition I felt it was as much for me, as it is for you. "There are many of us who do too much, keep too busy, spend all our time taking care of others and, in general, do not take care of ourselves. This is a book for women workaholics, busyaholics, rushaholics, and careaholics."

Obviously it's in your nature to want to help, which is a wonderful trait, but you will be better placed to meet (and greet) your responsibilities if you can prioritise and set boundaries.

Have we forgotten that we have a responsibility to ourselves to feel good? Now that's something that could go straight to the top of our lists.

Today's card has been drawn from the Miracle Cards. All material relating to the card and guidebook is copyright to Marianne Williamson, 2002.

November 13, 2015

Column 36: Surrender and achieve inner peace

THIS week a question was submitted anonymously: "My eldest son has moved away from home and when I visit him I get upset by how he's living. Should I say something?"

Based on today's card *Surrender* from Diana Cooper's *Angels of Light* deck, you have two choices: You can intervene and potentially jeopardise your relationship with your son or you can surrender.

It's ok to acknowledge that this situation upsets you. Family issues have a way of doing this. However, the message accompanying this indicates: "Whatever you resist in life persists." There comes a point when your awareness will show that a situation is keeping you 'stuck' and is robbing you of inner peace.

Parenting can feel like a minefield at the best of times. But if your child knows that you love and support them, there's not much more you can do. Making decisions for themselves is a necessary part of life. People learn from experience not from being told about experience.

My advice is not about burying your head in the sand, it's quite the contrary. It's about facing your feelings and letting go of the power that they have over you. When we have the desire to change other people's behaviours, we do so out of a belief that we will feel better. But, if we can feel better within ourselves, what we see outside of us will either no longer bother us or no longer matter.

It would be lackadaisical of me to highlight the issue

without providing at least a glimmer of hope or silver lining. So never fear, the solution is here in Master Eckhart Tolle. His answer is simple: "As soon as you honour the present moment, all unhappiness and struggle dissolve, and life begins to flow with joy and ease. When you act out the present-moment awareness, whatever you do becomes imbued with a sense of quality, care, and love – even the most simple action."

Tips on how to surrender and feel better now:

- ♥ Develop an inner strength so that no matter what happens you can convincingly say, "I'll handle it."
- ♥ Realise that this situation will help you clarify what it is you want from your life. This epitomises grace, which Tolle suggests is the doorway to the present moment.
- ♥ Acknowledge that each moment is an opportunity to be free, if you can allow it. Surrender equals freedom.

It's time to raise the white flag and relinquish control of anything you have no control over. Instead you'll have more time and energy to be present for *your* moments, whatever you wish them to be.

Today's card has been drawn from the Angels of Light Cards Pocket Edition. All material relating to the card is copyright to Diana Cooper, 2009.

November 20, 2015

SPECIAL EDITION for Walk A Mile In Her Shoes campaign: Take a stand for victims

At the outset, I would like to express my sincere condolences to the friends and relatives who have lost a loved one through violence.

Jill Meagher and Stephanie Scott have become household names in Australia…for all the wrong reasons. Their names are now synonymous with violence against women.

I sit before my computer wearing my yellow singlet, the one I bought the week of Stephanie's death (yellow is her remembrance colour). I'm hoping it will connect me with this sensitive and significant subject. It's one that has become all too familiar, featuring prominently in the headlines day after day.

A wave of emotion has come over me. It's similar to the unsettling feeling I had when, in a previous column, I attempted to articulate the impact that Stephanie Scott's death has had on the community.

Unfortunately, ours is one of many communities affected by violence against women and domestic violence at large. On September 23, media outlets reported that seven females had been killed every month of this year due to domestic violence. It came in the wake of a 12-year-old girl being murdered by her stepfather.

On September 30, *The Daily Advertiser* headlined with "End the Violence" in which a special report was dedicated to the scourge of domestic violence and a new "campaign aimed at addressing the attitudes and behaviours that contribute" to it.

Just days after being sworn in as Prime Minister, Malcolm

Turnbull touched on this critical subject declaring the level of violence against women a national disgrace. He insisted, "We have to make it as though it was un-Australian to disrespect women."

And in the aftermath of yet another mass shooting in the U.S., President Barack Obama uttered words which I couldn't help but relate to our own violent epidemic. He stated: "Somehow this has become routine. We have become numb to this."

Yet tragedies like the U.S. shooting and the deaths of Stephanie Scott and Jill Meagher should be anything but routine. The victims are not numbers or statistics, they were people with families and friends. They had real plans, real dreams, but unfortunately also real fears in their final moments. Lives cut short at the hands of another, for reasons we could never truly understand.

There is another household name that has appeared out of the darkness as a national torchbearer against violence. The cover of Rosie Batty's book, *A Mother's Story* says it all. "Heartache. Grief. Passion. Purpose." If she can turn such a tragic event into something positive, then surely so can we.

While writing this, the New South Wales State Government allocated $60 million, following the Federal Government's contribution of $100 million, to "tackle" domestic violence. Is it a case of something is better than nothing, even though we know more people will die from violence while these programs are rolled out? It seems we have a long way to go to help women feel safer and to change the attitudes of men who view violence as acceptable. However, there are ways to turn that helplessness into hope.

All around the country next Wednesday, men will be donning ladies shoes to raise awareness of this issue. It coincides with the United Nations' International Day for the Elimination of Violence Against Women. Thanks to the Griffith branch of Soroptimist International, the Walk A Mile In Her Shoes event will start at 12 noon at the car park opposite Rossies and finishing at the Memorial Gardens.

Fellas, don't let the lack of shoes in your size get in the way of a good cause. If they don't fit, flaunt them any way you can!

Another woman who was victim to violence, but has not become a household name is Carol Penrith. She was killed in Griffith in November 2014, just five months before Stephanie Scott was killed in nearby Leeton. Yet, Carol's death was not as public. Her attacker (Carol's de-facto at the time) is now behind bars serving a minimum of 13-years for murder. In October 2016, Vincent Stanford was sentenced to life in prison for the murder and sexual assault of Stephanie Scott.

There are many other victims that I have not named, but that doesn't make their deaths any less significant. This article was my attempt to continue generating awareness of an issue that plagues our communities daily.

♥ This week's special edition column also appeared in *The Daily Advertiser* as a hot topic.

November 27, 2015

Column 37: Pressure is "self-imposed"

THIS week a question was submitted anonymously: "I recently read your article on surrender. I know that's what I need to do, but I'm struggling with people expecting more and more from me. Some advice would really help."

Today's card *Burdens* courtesy of Colette Baron-Reid is about contemplating the nature of the burdens we carry. The key message is that it's "time to leave behind any unnecessary burdens and to know you have the strength to carry what's yours." But to get to that realisation we must first acknowledge what we consider our burdens to be.

There's no shortage of potential burdens these days. People and events constantly require our attention. We deal with one and then before we can catch our breath, there's another, and another. Unfortunately, that feeling of being overwhelmed and overcommitted seems to be the norm for many.

Helping others, doing things for others, often becomes second nature to us. Mothers are quick to engage in this behaviour, for obvious reasons. Admirable? Sure. Exhausting? Most definitely!

Many self-help books advise to lay down your burdens. Maybe it's not a case of where you lay them down but to whom? Delegation springs to mind. What "burdens" have you taken upon yourself that actually belong to someone else? It might be as minor as picking up after a family member or as major as caring for an elderly parent.

In her bestseller, *The Yo-Yo Diet Syndrome*, Doreen Virtue

makes connections between weight and behaviour (but that's a whole other column!). For today, her sentiment about burdens is direct but also empowering. She writes: "All pressure and stress is self-imposed. We decide on our stress levels through our mental outlook, by saying yes when we want to say no, and by making decisions about our jobs, relationships, and other life areas out of guilt and fear – instead of out of love. Fortunately, if we don't like the results of our past choices, we can choose again."

Tips on how to NOT become a beast of burden:

♥ Identify your major tasks and responsibilities. Writing them down will help to see the breadth of your burdens.

♥ Review your to-do list – are you doing more than your fair share? Are there things on your list that aren't really necessary?

♥ Juggling commitments and prioritising are naturally part of a busy lifestyle. So delegate or delete anything that's crept onto your plate that isn't yours or is no longer meaningful to you.

Think of this as an exercise in evaluating your whole life. I suspect it represents a bigger transformation than you might be aware of. A caterpillar might look at its cocoon as a restriction, the contents of the pupa might look like an oozy mess, but as we all know after this radical transformation emerges a butterfly.

Today's card has been drawn from The Wisdom of Avalon Oracle Cards. All material relating to the card and guidebook is copyright to Colette Baron-Reid, 2007.

♥ *Colette Baron-Reid liked and commented on this post on Facebook by saying, "This is wonderful congratulations Sharon Halliday."*

December 4, 2015

Column 38: Cherish every experience

THIS week Kay asks: "My friends and family don't know how much I'd like to be doing something different with my life. It's hard to focus on everyday stuff when I want to be doing my art. So what do I do?"

"Are we there yet?" Four words that can raise the hackles of any parent travelling with children. Unfortunately this 'not enjoying the journey' syndrome is not limited to children.

Our lives are so full and busy, but not necessarily with the things we love doing. We experience glimpses and glimmers of happiness, fun and enthusiasm instead of having it in spades.

There are two parts to answering your question. One is about going out of your comfort zone to pursue something that is close to your heart and the other is about enjoying the journey in the meantime.

My homepage features the *Travelling* card with words from the *Osho Zen Tarot*. "The tiny figure moving on the path through this beautiful landscape is not concerned about the goal. He or she knows that the journey is the goal; the pilgrimage itself is the sacred place. Each step on the path is important in itself."

That's all well and good for the "tiny figure" depicted on the card, but how do we share that same sense of trust?

Lately I've written a lot about how to lighten the load so that we can enjoy this journey we call life. A key to making the "everyday stuff" more palatable is to ensure that you're spending time doing things that are meaningful (not just because your head says they are, but because your heart is in it).

To overcome your quandary, taking time-out from the daily grind for your creative pursuits is something you might need to get accustomed to. Certainly, if you have identified your art as your life purpose, then even more reason to integrate it into your daily life. You'll be following your bliss!

Today's *Adventure* card, from Denise Linn's *Soul Coaching Oracle Cards*, will give you even more confidence that the mundane can become memorable. It looks at the journey as one of anticipation and excitement. In the guidebook accompanying this card, Denise writes: "Adventure entails risks, and without them, existence can become stagnant and lacklustre. If your life seems uninspired in some areas, be willing to take risks and try something new."

Tips on how to find joy in the journey:

♥ A journey is made up of many small steps. Some action towards your goal is better than nothing; before you know it momentum will build.

♥ Emulate the feeling of having already arrived at your goal. Find things in your existing landscape to celebrate.

♥ Be passionate about your passion. Purchase tools, start dabbling, research – do whatever it takes to immerse yourself in it.

♥ When it comes to outside influences, try not to worry about what your friends and family think of your new pursuits, after all this is *your* life. You might be pleasantly surprised by how much interest and support you receive from them.

Despite being a huge fan, I never thought I'd be quoting from Aerosmith to make a point, but their song "Amazing" reminds us all that, "Life's a journey not a destination."

The *"Travelling"* card was selected from the Osho Zen Tarot: The Transcendental Game of Zen. All material relating to the card and guidebook is copyright to Osho International Foundation Switzerland, 1995.

Today's card has been drawn from the Soul Coaching Oracle Cards: What Your Soul Wants You to Know. All material relating to the card and guidebook is copyright to Denise Linn, 2006.

♥ Denise Linn liked and commented on this post on Facebook by saying, *"I love the company I'm with!"*

December 11, 2015

Column 39: Don't ever give up on your dreams

TOMORROW marks one year of weekly Ask Sharon columns for *The Area News*.

My brother loaned me a book. It's signed by the author, Australian actor, stuntman and success coach Kurek Ashley. Inside the cover of *How Would Love Respond?* is scrawled "Live Your Dreams!" A simple and powerful message. But then I asked why. Why are dreams so important?

Fast-forward to page 177 and Kurek answers my question. He writes: "When people give up on their dreams, they become zombies. The spark of life is missing from their eyes. Your body might still be walking around, but your spirit is dead because your soul is trapped in a vehicle that has thrown away the best part of human experience."

As I was contemplating the direction of my own dreams, Australia was embracing our first female jockey to win the Melbourne Cup. I'll admit it, when Michelle Payne beat the odds not only at the track but also in life on that historic occasion, I cried.

Michelle mentioned that the night before, she considered what she would say if she won. At first she thought, "Don't be silly" but concluded, "It's nice to be able to dream." That's when the floodgates opened. I feel very passionate about people pursuing their dreams. And now I'm about to pursue mine.

One year ago, two mums were sitting at the local aquatic centre watching their kids play, unaware that their sons were best friends at preschool. They began chatting about parenthood, careers and invariably, how to juggle the two!

Then one mum leaned in and asked the other, "Would you like to write for the paper?" The other mum responded eagerly, "Where do I sign?"

And so what began as two mums exchanging ideas has developed into a beautiful friendship. Thank you Monique Patterson for taking a chance on me. I am truly grateful for the opportunity…and our friendship.

To the people who have read my columns and stopped me in the street to pass on their feedback – thank you. My main goal with my writing is to either make people think or smile. If it has done both then I am a happy little vegemite. But as I write this, my last column, and turn my attention to producing my first book, I feel ready to live *my* dream.

Whether we admit it or not, each of us has something inside of us, a special purpose that is our unique calling. It doesn't matter if it's a desire to become a published author like me, or be the winner of the Melbourne Cup, like Michelle Payne.

So I'll leave you with one last tip as I heed the advice of the late Wayne Dyer – one of the most influential spiritual leaders of our time – "Don't die with your music still in you."

♥ *This post was liked and shared on Facebook by Kurek Ashley.*

♥ *The tweet about this column was liked on Twitter by Michelle Payne.*

A Final Word

Although I officially finished my columns as Ask Sharon on December 11, 2015 I wrote an additional column for International Women's Day in 2016.

March 4, 2016

SPECIAL EDITION for International Women's Day: Trailblazers pave the way for women

THERE seems to be an international day for just about everything, but there is one I'll be paying homage to. Next Tuesday is International Women's Day, and according to the United Nations it's "a time to reflect on progress made, to call for change and to celebrate acts of courage and determination by ordinary women who have played an extraordinary role in the history of their countries and communities."

In Griffith the occasion will be celebrated with a breakfast on Friday 11 March hosted by the local branch of Soroptimist International – an organisation which is "a global voice for women."

In the invitation to the event I read about guest speaker Jane Caro. Jane is a "renowned author, social commentator, columnist, broadcaster and award winning advertising writer. Jane appears frequently on Sunrise, Q&A, The Project and The Gruen Transfer. She is also the mother of two daughters, a wife, a beef producer and a timber grower. By her own admission, Jane has a low boredom threshold."

That last bit gave me a wry smile as it resonated loud and clear. I too have a low boredom threshold. I immediately began concocting possible questions I would ask Jane should I get the opportunity. "How do you do it?" was at the forefront.

The moment I printed my own ticket for the breakfast (very 21st century), there was an ensuing brain-frenzy. My thoughts raced to school drop-off, homework obligations, uniforms, lunch orders…My hands were equally as frantic reaching for post-it notes and a pen that worked to relay all the instructions.

Now, while my hubby is more than capable of taking care of the kids on his own, suddenly getting a six-year old to school on time with a toddler in tow, put it into another category (at least in my mind). I wondered, is this my issue of control or a representation of what is expected of women who work and raise a family in the new millennium?

It got me thinking further about this (sometimes lofty) concept of work-life balance. The topic is a subjective one. One woman's norm is another's nightmare! Regardless, what really matters is that a woman is happy – whatever she is doing – even if it is more of a juggling act than a balancing act at times.

So while we haven't yet found the magic formula for achieving work-life balance (very un-21st century), it doesn't really matter.

What I do know is that as long as there are extraordinary women like Jane blazing new trails, and organisations like Soroptimist International supporting women, we'll be ok.

I was lucky enough to speak with Jane after the breakfast. As she signed a copy of her book, *Plain-Speaking Jane*, I asked her my question about how she tackles parenting and a career. Interestingly, her response, which she wrote on the inside cover was, "Just do less."

Sharon met Jane Caro, author of *Plain-Speaking Jane* at Griffith's International Women's Day Breakfast in 2016.

Index

109

List of angel and oracle cards consulted by Ask Sharon

Column 1: Should I stay or should I go?
"Communicating Freely", "Following Your Bliss", and "Being in the Flow" from the *Gateway Oracle Cards* by Denise Linn. Published by Hay House, 2012.

Column 2: Time to let go of negativity
"Forgiveness Heals", "Detoxification", and "Unconditional Joy" from the *Archangel Raphael Healing Oracle Cards* by Doreen Virtue. Published by Hay House, 2010.

Column 3: Mary seeks advice on life
"Fulfillment" from the *Soul Coaching Oracle Cards: What Your Soul Wants You to Know* by Denise Linn. Published by Hay House, 2006.

Column 4: Messages from above
"I send you loving signs through nature" from the *Talking to Heaven Mediumship Cards* by Doreen Virtue and James Van Praagh. Published by Hay House, 2013.

Column 5: Trust that it will all work out
"Trust" from the *Osho Zen Tarot: The Transcendental Game of Zen* by Osho. Published by Boxtree, 1994.

Column 6: Tap into your own inner truth
"Inspiration" from the *Soul Coaching Oracle Cards: What Your Soul Wants You to Know* by Denise Linn. Published by Hay House, 2006.

Column 7 (part one): Respect the key to success
"Self-Respect" from the *Archangel Michael Oracle Cards* by Doreen Virtue. Published by Hay House, 2009.

Column 7 (part two): Be kind to yourself and other people
"Self-Respect" from the *Archangel Michael Oracle Cards* by Doreen Virtue. Published by Hay House, 2009.

Column 8: Appreciate what you have in life
"Appreciation" from *Money and the Law of Attraction Cards* by Esther and Jerry Hicks. Published by Hay House, 2009.

Column 9: Don't ignore issues in life
"Accepting What Is" from the *Gateway Oracle Cards* by Denise Linn. Published by Hay House, 2012.

Column 10: Embrace life's challenges
"New Beginnings" from the *Archangel Power Tarot Cards* by Doreen Virtue and Radleigh Valentine. Published by Hay House, 2013.

Column 11: Enjoy every waking hour
"Following Your Bliss" from the *Gateway Oracle Cards* by Denise Linn. Published by Hay House, 2012.

Column 12: Treat your body as a friend to lose weight
"Ask Your Body for a Message" from the *Archangel Raphael Healing Oracle Cards* by Doreen Virtue. Published by Hay House, 2010.

SPECIAL EDITION for the Murder of Leeton School Teacher and Bride-to-Be Stephanie Scott: Time to show compassion

"Life and Death" from the *Miracle Cards* by Marianne Williamson. Published by Hay House, 2002.

Column 13: Releasing yourself from the to-do list
"Be Gentle with Yourself" from the *Archangel Michael Oracle Cards* by Doreen Virtue. Published by Hay House, 2009.

Column 14: Don't sweat small stuff
"Wait" from the *Angel Answers Oracle Cards* by Doreen Virtue and Radleigh Valentine. Published by Hay House, 2014.

SPECIAL EDITION for Mother's Day (part two): Cherish time spent with your child
"Totality" from the *Osho Zen Tarot: The Transcendental Game of Zen* by Osho. Published by Boxtree, 1994.

Column 15: Take time to enjoy simple pleasures
"Savouring Pleasure" from the *Gateway Oracle Cards* by Denise Linn. Published by Hay House, 2012.

Column 16: Our dreams may contain messages
"Key" from the *Fortune Reading Cards* by Sharina Star. Published by Rockpool Publishing, 2015.

Column 17: As the bard said, be true to yourself
"Admit the Truth to Yourself and Act Accordingly" from the *Archangel Michael Oracle Cards* by Doreen Virtue. Published by Hay House, 2009.

Column 18: Be open to unlimited possibilities
"Possibilities" from the *Osho Zen Tarot: The Transcendental Game of Zen* by Osho. Published by Boxtree, 1994.

Column 19: A reminder to have fun!
"Laughter Is the Best Medicine" from the *Archangel Raphael Healing Oracle Cards* by Doreen Virtue. Published by Hay House, 2010.

Column 20: Positive thinking powerful
"My Thoughts Are in Harmony with Health" from *The Law of Attraction Cards* by Esther and Jerry Hicks. Published by Hay House, 2008.

Column 21: Embrace your authenticity
"Artistic Expression" from the *Ascended Masters Oracle Cards* by Doreen Virtue. Published by Hay House, 2007.

Column 22: Always live in the moment
"Focus" from the *Soul Coaching Oracle Cards: What Your Soul Wants You to Know* by Denise Linn. Published by Hay House, 2006.

Column 23 (part one): Parenthood a constant juggling act
"Compassion" from the *Goddess Guidance Oracle Cards* by Doreen Virtue. Published by Hay House, 2004.

Column 23 (part two): Ask Sharon – Let it go
"Let it go" from the *Ascended Masters Oracle Cards* by Doreen Virtue. Published by Hay House, 2007.

Column 24: Sharon says listen to your wise voice
"Listening" from the *Self-Care Cards* by Cheryl Richardson. Published by Hay House, 2001.

Column 25: We must embrace change

"Transformation" from the *Soul Coaching Oracle Cards: What Your Soul Wants You to Know* by Denise Linn. Published by Hay House, 2006.

Column 26: Our dreams have meaning
"You're Ready" from the *Angel Answers Oracle Cards* by Doreen Virtue and Radleigh Valentine. Published by Hay House, 2014.

Column 27: Don't rush your recovery
"Door to Spirit" from the *Energy Oracle Cards* by Sandra Anne Taylor. Published by Hay House, 2013.

Column 28: Remember the big picture
"Focus" from *The Wisdom of Avalon Oracle Cards* by Colette Baron-Reid. Published by Hay House, 2007.

Column 29: Take time to reach out to loved ones
"Mending Bridges" from the *Gateway Oracle Cards* by Denise Linn. Published by Hay House, 2012.

Column 30: Declutter for superior sleep
"Renewing Your Life" from the *Gateway Oracle Cards* by Denise Linn. Published by Hay House, 2012.

Column 31: You don't have to follow along
"Conditioning" from the *Osho Zen Tarot: The Transcendental Game of Zen* by Osho. Published by Boxtree, 1994.

Column 32: Loved ones want to help
"Help" from the *Self-Care Cards* by Cheryl Richardson. Published by Hay House, 2001.

Column 33 (part one): True love can be magical
"Opening to Love" from the *Gateway Oracle Cards* by Denise Linn. Published by Hay House, 2012.

Column 34 (Halloween Special): Release the skeletons in the closet
"You Can Do It" from the *Ascended Masters Oracle Cards* by Doreen Virtue. Published by Hay House, 2007.

Column 35: Don't overcommit yourself
"Personal Power" from the *Miracle Cards* by Marianne Williamson. Published by Hay House, 2002.

Column 36: Surrender and achieve inner peace
"Surrender" from the *Angels of Light Cards Pocket Edition* by Diana Cooper. Published by Findhorn Press, 2009.

Column 37: Pressure is "self-imposed"
"Burdens" from *The Wisdom of Avalon Oracle Cards* by Colette Baron-Reid. Published by Hay House, 2007.

Column 38: Cherish every experience
"Travelling" from the *Osho Zen Tarot: The Transcendental Game of Zen* by Osho. Published by Boxtree, 1994.

"Adventure" from the *Soul Coaching Oracle Cards: What Your Soul Wants You to Know* by Denise Linn. Published by Hay House, 2006.

Some of the Ask Sharon columns, as they appeared in The Area News

Are you looking for a little guidance? Sharon Halliday, a Certified Angel Intuitive, answers your questions.

Time to let go of negativity

This week Claire asks: *Once again I've over-indulged at Christmas. I usually find it takes me a while to recover. What can I do differently?*

Today I was drawn to Doreen Virtue's Archangel Raphael Healing Oracle Cards. The first card was "Forgiveness Heals". You might think, "What has forgiveness got to do with over-indulgence?" But honestly, there could not have been a more accurate card to represent the source of the issue. It is about replacing toxic emotions with peace and health. When you are angry with yourself or others, it is you who suffers. This card symbolises that it is time to let go of past negative experiences and emotions that have been stored in your mind, heart and body. You may be pleasantly surprised by how much physical and emotional baggage you let go of by allowing yourself to forgive.

The second card was "Detoxification." It doesn't mean you have to buy a program or pills, quite the opposite. A detox can be as simple as refining what and how you eat and drink (without judgement). It can be about moderation as opposed to cutting entire things out. It can be reducing some things you consume and increasing others (you will have an instinct about what these are already). It can be starting your day with some fresh lemon juice in a glass of water to kick-start your metabolism. Do explore what detoxification means to you, but I am getting a strong sense that this card's message will ring true

because it is something you have considered for some time. Take it slowly, enjoy the process by looking at it as an act of self-love. When you begin to take care of any aspect of yourself, your effort will be rewarded by how you feel within. The outer effects will be the icing on the cake (no pun intended).

The final card, which can represent the result of acting on the other two, is "Unconditional Joy". It also highlights that it is possible to attain joy right now regardless of your circumstances. I can see two quick ways to get you on the path of joy. Firstly, give yourself a break from judgement. When you continue a behaviour and then judge or berate yourself for it, you will stay stuck in a dysfunctional cycle. When you acknowledge that what you've been doing in over-indulging is an attempt to soothe yourself and fill a void with something (like food or alcohol), you can begin a process of empowerment and be open to positive choices. This will lighten the load and allow joy to re-enter your life.

Secondly, be grateful for everything you have in your life now.

You could obtain a nice crystal, but a rock will do. Place in your pocket and throughout your day when you notice it, be thankful for anything and everything you can think of.

This can be a powerful practice. You can be thankful for anything from your family, your home to a flower or a breeze.

Send your questions for Sharon to editor@areanews.com.au

126

Messages from above

THIS week Louise asks: I want to believe that the feelings I've had lately are my friends and relatives who have passed, but sometimes it makes me miss them more.

This is an area that is close to my heart, as it is for many.

To answer your inquiry, I consulted the Talking to Heaven mediumship cards by Doreen Virtue and James Van Praagh.

I knew that any of their cards would offer you relief, but the one that revealed itself was "I send you loving signs through nature".

This was the perfect card to bring you comfort and provide clarity for your feelings.

Only recently I was not sure how to interpret signs that I felt were coming from above.

I came across a CD featuring a song that played at my friend's memorial, then an old magazine – the cover story featured bowel cancer, which she died from.

I send you loving signs through nature.

I knew I could no longer ignore that she was trying to communicate with me. My grief had been blinding me from seeing and feeling her signs.

Sometimes our rational mind gets in the way of our faith. It is our heart that needs to guide us to that inner knowing, especially when we have no tangible proof.

It is out of the unknown and unexplainable that our faith is reborn.

When you are feeling doubtful about the validity of signs, ask yourself what brings you more hope? What causes you to feel better? To shut yourself off from the idea that those who are no longer on earth are connecting with you or to notice and trust the signs that your loved ones are still with you?

I believe one of the reasons our loved ones pass is because they can be of more service to us in heaven than on earth.

I encourage you to be open to the signs. They come to bring you comfort, peace, understanding and guidance.

This passage from the Talking to Heaven guidebook highlights the message for you today from your deceased loved ones: "We've sent you birds, dragonflies, butterflies, flowers, clouds, and rainbows.

"Each time you notice these signs, your body gives you confirmation of who sent them to you."

Send your questions for Sharon to editor@area news.com.au.

– SHARON HALLIDAY

127

MOTHER AND DAUGHTER: The mother of all ways to say thank you" is with a card this Sunday ...or is it?

Show Mum you care on Mother's Day

THIS week the sea of pink and excessive use of the word 'special' prompted me to recall conversations I've had with my mummy friends.

One of them had asked, "Does Mother's Day really mean anything anyway?"

I began digging.

Mother's Day was founded by American Anna Jarvis to honour her own and other mothers as 'the person who has done more for you than anyone in the world".

When Mother's Day was proclaimed as a national holiday in 1914, it wasn't long before certain card-making companies began cashing in.

"Jarvis's intention for the holiday had been for people to appreciate and honour mothers by writing a personal letter, by hand, expressing love and gratitude, rather than buying gifts and pre-made cards."

So what does all this mean to modern mothers?

Are they prepared to trade the fluffy slippers and a sleep-in (well, maybe not the sleep-in) for a hand-made card and a thank you?

Most mothers embrace the mother of all roles with gusto but somewhere along the way of nappies, nap times and Nanna naps (if we're

ASK SHARON

lucky!) we can lose ourselves.

We can even lose our identity, our freedom and for some, our dress sense - flats over heels is no longer a choice but a necessity.

So what's the key to showing mum how much she is appreciated for her dedication?

Sincerity. And it can come in many forms.

Tips on how to uphold the true sentiment of Mother's Day - Jarvis-style:

- Help, help and more help but without being asked - with great gestures comes great recognition!

- Compassion - a little understanding can go a long way.

- Support her dreams. In Buddhism this is referred to

as sympathetic joy. It's a two-way street kind of notion, so let's revisit it when Father's Day rolls around.

- Anything you can do to help 'mum' honour her own needs will be well received (never underestimate the value of uninterrupted bathroom time).

- If in doubt, act from love.

Given the significance of the motherhood issue, next week I'll be delving deeper into how mothers can reclaim their sanity and sense of self the other 364 days of the year.

Send your questions for Sharon to editor@areanews.com.au

ARE you looking for a little guidance? Sharon Halliday, a Griffith resident, is a Certified Angel Intuitive who offers oracle and angel card readings.

The cards are a lighthearted and playful approach to receiving guidance - and we can all do with a bit of that at times in our lives. Yet they can also have a powerful effect and it is always positive.

The guidance can cover a range of subjects, from relationships to attracting more money, to healthy lifestyle changes and discovering your life purpose.

Be open to unlimited possibilities

BY SHARON HALLIDAY

THIS week Scott asked: *I don't believe in much, I don't even read my horoscope so what could your cards possibly tell someone like me?*

Well, the cards and the guidance they represent can tell you quite a lot. The issue is how much of it will permeate your being, in this non-believer state that you mention.

Even saying the words that come naturally to me, "I'll tune into your question as I shuffle the cards", would cause you to feel what I refer to as resistance.

In other words, it will stir within you more annoyance and irritation than bring a sense of appeasement.

Yet, I believe today's card from the OSHO Zen Tarot, "Possibilities", is the best place to start.

I'll admit, it's not some earth-shattering epiphany-like card, but it is what you're looking for – even if you don't yet believe it!

I have to be honest and say, I was relieved that the cards "Letting Go" or "Consciousness" didn't emerge, as that might further drive you away from a world of possibilities. However, the

Ask Sharon

thing about card readings is that they are often a highly accurate measure of what is going on in someone's life and they provide gentle and reassuring guidance... always.

Tips on how to be open to possibilities:
■ Start with the little things – can you at least bring yourself to appreciate a meal, a sunset, your paycheck?
■ Ask yourself, "What's the worst that can happen, if just for a while, I make an attempt to look beyond what it is I think I know?"
■ Consider that life is meant to deliver more to you than the mediocre and that the key to that life is in your hands.

I don't believe you can go from being a non-believer one day to having an unshakable faith the next – at least not without the help of a near death experience or some major life event (aka a wake-up call).

But don't take my word for it. I refer to a passage that accompanied the "Possibilities" card.

"Those who remain content easily remain small: small are their joys, small are their ecstasies, small are their silences, small is their being. But there is no need! This smallness is your own imposition upon your freedom, upon your unlimited possibilities, upon your unlimited potential."

As you go about your life, I hope that you might recall this exchange and at some point recognise that all it takes is to open your eyes even the slightest to be aware of opportunities and your potential.

Something may happen that makes your non-believer status a thing of the past and your life will never be the same again. It could be better than you ever imagined.

Send your questions for Sharon to *editor@areanews. com.au*

Sharon says listen to your wise voice

BY SHARON HALLIDAY

THIS week Jane asked: *"I'm not unwell but I'm living in a fog, going from one thing to the next. How can I shake this fuzzy feeling?"*

One could easily be mistaken for thinking this week's column would be all about seeing more clearly, yet it was the "listening" card that appeared from Cheryl Richardson's Self-Care deck.

While this card's message is to, "listen to your wise self", I felt there was much more to it than just being guided by your inner voice.

When I was growing up, the phrase, "they could talk underwater with a mouthful of marbles" was thrown around a lot...usually in my direction! I admit it, I like to talk...a lot (my husband would certainly vouch for this). Maybe it was originally an attention-seeking thing, maybe it was an immaturity thing, but regardless it took me a while to learn that an important part of communication is to listen to others. It took me even longer to learn to listen to my "wise inner self".

I feel that you are at a place in your life where your next course of action is to listen. Listen and be guided by your instincts without the second-guessing and without the seeking of opinions from others. This is about you and your valid inner nudges. I'll bet you've tried everything else, and that explains the fuzziness that has probably become all-too familiar to you.

ASK SHARON: Sharon Halliday: "be aware that the big pay-off from listening to your inner self is the inspiration that always proceeds." Picture: Supplied.

Another familiarity that doesn't serve us well is the way we communicate. How often do you find yourself in a conversation with someone and you are already thinking about what you are going to say next without really listening? We all do it. But we are also missing out on being present, being engaged and being exposed to relevant information that might be the very thing to clear our path.

Signs can come in all forms including things that other people say. Often, many of my serendipity moments come via a statement made by someone else. Why does this synchronicity even matter? Because not only does it feel exhilarating when that moment happens, but it confirms loud and clear that I am on the right path.

It is these moments of inspiration that will guide you out of the fog.

Send your questions for Sharon to *editor@areanews. com.au*

NEWS

Advice for mothers

Ask Sharon: Let it go

BY SHARON HALLIDAY

LAST week Maria asked: I work a lot then when I'm at home I'm busy doing all the other stuff that has to get done. I worry that my kids are missing out?

For part two of this mammoth question. I shuffled the cards from a different deck to last week, and amazingly received the same Ascended Master Quan Yin! Except instead of "Compassion', the card was "Let It Go", which again helps guide the advice on this important issue for parents and particularly mums.

I was discussing this subject with another mother recently and my feeling was that our kids are not likely to reminisce and say, "I wish mum had cleaned the floor more" but they might say, "I wish she'd got down on the floor and played with me more!"

This is not about compounding any feelings of guilt, but rather to give you a sense of perspective about the 'other stuff'. I've resigned to the fact that while my kids are young, these will not be the years I can claim the cleanest house. I do the bare minimum...the supermum in me died long ago!

So today's column is about making peace with where you are in your life and seeing where you can release the unimportant to make room

for the things that matter.

Tips on how to loosen the reins and let go.

· Let go of the common misperception of feeling guilty when you're not with your children.

· Let go of your own standards and expectations, they will only cause stress and frustration.

· Let go of the housework and anything that can wait.

There's a poster which sums that last point up the best, "Good mums have sticky floors, messy kitchens, laundry piles, dirty ovens and happy kids." And just in case I still haven't hit home, I went back to Ita Buttrose's

ASK SHARON: Ita Buttrose said: "Society not only puts a lot of pressure on working mums, but women put unrealistic pressures on themselves as well." Send your questions for Sharon to editor@areanows.com.au

Motherguilt. She writes, "Sometimes in their haste to get through all of the things they have to do, working mothers forget some of the most important things in life - like living, for instance. Mothers do not have to be perfect, good enough will do."

My new philosophy in

achieving something that resembles a work/life balance goes beyond domesticity. I've stopped being so quick to clip my own wings when it comes to the parenting department. Instead I now recognise, like all well-meaning parents, that what we are aiming to do is give children wings so they can fly.

Your soul mate will find you
True love can be magical

OPEN YOUR HEART: Only when you truly love yourself will you be open to true love, says columnist Sharon Halliday. Picture & art: art.ao photography

---

Cherish precious moments

PRECIOUS TIME: Columnist Sharon Halliday encourages fathers to spend as much time with their children as possible. Picture: b.art.ao photography

Bibliography

Column 6: Tap into your own inner truth
Yoga Horizons 2016, accessed 9 February 2015, http://www.yogahorizons.biz/quotes.html

Column 7 (part two): Be kind to yourself and other people
AZ Quotes 2017, accessed 23 February 2015, http://www.azquotes.com/quote/814852

Column 9: Don't ignore issues in life
Williamson, M., (2010). *A Course in Weight Loss: 21 spiritual lessons for surrendering your weight forever.* Sydney: Hay House.

Column 10: Embrace life's challenges
Hay, L., (1999). *Power Thought Cards.* Carlsbad: Hay House.

Column 10: Embrace life's challenges
Goodreads 2017, accessed 16 March 2015, https://www.goodreads.com/author/quotes/20105.Joseph_Campbell.

Column 11: Enjoy every waking hour
Hicks, E.&J., (2009). *The Vortex: Where the Law of Attraction Assembles All Cooperative Relationships.* Sydney: Hay House.

Column 12: Treat your body as a friend to lose weight
Chopra Center Meditation 2017, accessed 6 April 2015, https://www.chopra.com

SPECIAL EDITION for the Murder of Leeton School Teacher and Bride-to-Be Stephanie Scott: Time to show compassion
Abraham–Hicks 2017, accessed 12 April 2015, http://www.abraham-hicks.com/lawofattractionsource/about_abraham.php

Column 13: Releasing yourself from the to-do list
Hicks, E.&J., (2008). *Manifest Your Desires: 365 Ways to Make Your Dreams a Reality.* Carlsbad: Hay House

Column 14: Don't sweat small stuff
Carlson, K. (2001). *Don't Sweat the Small Stuff for Women: Simple and Practical Ways to Do What Matters Most and Find Time for You.* New York: Hyperion.

SPECIAL EDITION for Mother's Day (part one): Show Mum you care on Mother's Day
Wikipedia 2017, accessed 2 May 2015, https://en.wikipedia.org/wiki/Mother's_Day

Column 15: Take time to enjoy simple pleasures
Hay, L., (2014). *Loving Yourself to Great Health: Thoughts & Food – the Ultimate Diet.* Sydney: Hay House.

Column 15: Take time to enjoy simple pleasures
Forbes 2017, accessed 19 May 2015, https://www.forbes.com/sites/travisbradberry/2015/03/24/how-successful-people-spend-their-weekends/#74207ddc19c0

Column 16: Our dreams may contain messages
Leon Nacson 2017, accessed 26 May 2015, http://www.dreamcoach.com.au/emotions.aspx

Column 17: As the bard said, be true to yourself
Moorjani, A., (2012). *Dying to be Me: My journey from cancer, to near death, to true healing.* Sydney: Hay House.

Column 17: As the bard said, be true to yourself
Wiktionary 2017, accessed 2 June 2015, https://en.wiktionary. org/wiki/to_thine_own_self_be_true

Column 19: A reminder to have fun!
Abraham-Hicks 2017, accessed 16 June 2015, http:// www.abraham-hicks.com/lawofattractionsource/about_ abraham.php

Column 20: Positive thinking powerful
Harper, C., (2010). *Stop F*cking Around!: 30 principles for a better life (self-help for people who hate self-help).* Melbourne: Craig Harper.

Column 21: Embrace your authenticity
Sharma, R., (2004). *Discover Your Destiny With The Monk Who Sold His Ferrari: The 7 Stages of Self-Awakening.* London: HarperCollins Publishers.

Column 22: Always live in the moment
Brainy Quote 2017, accessed 6 July 2015, https://www. brainyquote.com/quotes/quotes/b/bilkeane121860.html

Column 22: Always live in the moment
Eckhart Tolle 2017, accessed 7 July 2015, https://www. eckharttolle.com/

Column 23 (part one): Parenthood a constant juggling act
Buttrose, I. & Adams, P., (2005). *Motherguilt: Australian women reveal their true feelings about motherhood.* Melbourne: Penguin.

Column 23 (part two): Ask Sharon – Let it go
Play With Your Family 2017, accessed 20 July 2015, http://www.playwithyourfamily.com/2011/09/good-moms-have-sticky-floors/

Column 23 (part two): Ask Sharon – Let it go
Buttrose, I. & Adams, P., (2005). *Motherguilt: Australian women reveal their true feelings about motherhood.* Melbourne: Penguin.

Column 25: We must embrace change
Goodreads 2017, accessed 2 August 2015, https://www.goodreads.com/quotes/2043-the-snake-which-cannot-cast-its-skin-has-to-die

Column 25: We must embrace change
Quotations Page 2017, accessed 2 August 2015, http://www.quotationspage.com/quote/26032.html

Column 26: Our dreams have meaning
Inserra, R., (2002) *Dictionary of Dreams: Understanding dreams & their messages.* Melbourne: Hinkler Books.

Column 27: Don't rush your recovery
Choquette, S., (2011). *The Power of Your Spirit: A Guide to Joyful Living.* 2nd ed. Sydney: Hay House.

Column 28: Remember the big picture
Richardson, C. (2000). *Take Time for Your Life: A Seven-Step Programme for Creating the Life You Want.* London: Bantam.

SPECIAL EDITION for Father's Day (part one): Take time to show your dad you care
Wikipedia 2017, accessed 1 September 2015, https://en.wikipedia.org/wiki/Father's_Day

SPECIAL EDITION for Father's Day (part two): Cherish precious moments
Wikipedia 2017, accessed 8 September 2015, http://www.drphil.com/advice/the-role-of-the-man-in-the-family/

Column 29: Take time to reach out to loved ones
Holden, R., (2009) *Success Intelligence: Essential Lessons and Practices from the World's Leading Coaching Program on Authentic Success.* 3rd ed. Carlsbad: Hay House.

Column 30: Declutter for superior sleep
Wikiquote 2017, accessed 20 September 2015, https://en.wikiquote.org/wiki/Fight_Club_(novel)

Column 32: Loved ones want to help
AZLyrics 2017, accessed 5 October 2015, http://www.azlyrics.com/lyrics/beatles/help.html

Column 33 (part one): True love can be magical
Gray, J. (1993) *Men Are from Mars, Women Are from Venus: A Practical Guide for Improving Communication and Getting What You Want in Your Relationships.* London: Thorsons.

Column 33 (part two): Self-love the key to happiness
Hay, L., (1999) *You Can Heal Your Life.* Gift ed. Carlsbad: Hay House.

Column 34 (Halloween Special): Release the skeletons in the closet
Jeffers, S., (1987). *Feel the Fear and Do It Anyway: How to Turn Your Fear and Indecision Into Confidence and Action.* London: Arrow Books.

Column 35: Don't overcommit yourself
Schaef, A.W., (2004). *Meditations for Women Who Do Too Much.* New York: HarperCollins Publishers.

Column 36: Surrender and achieve inner peace
Goodreads 2017, accessed 9 November 2015, https://www.goodreads.com/quotes/143211-as-soon-as-you-honor-the-present-moment-all-unhappiness

SPECIAL EDITION for Walk A Mile In Her Shoes campaign: Take a stand for victims
Smith, E, 2015. End the Cycle. *The Daily Advertiser,* 30 September 2015.

SPECIAL EDITION for Walk A Mile In Her Shoes campaign: Take a stand for victims
ABC 2017, accessed 15 November 2015, http://www.abc.net.au/pm/content/2015/s4319196.htm

SPECIAL EDITION for Walk A Mile In Her Shoes campaign: Take a stand for victims
Batty, R., (2015). *A Mother's Story.* Sydney: HarperCollins Publishers.

Column 37: Pressure is "self-imposed"
Virtue, D., (1997). *The Yo-Yo Diet Syndrome: How to Heal and Stabilize Your Appetite and Weight.* Carlsbad: Hay House.

Column 38: Cherish every experience
AZLyrics 2017, accessed 1 December 2015, http://www. azlyrics.com/lyrics/aerosmith/amazing.html

Column 39: Don't ever give up on your dreams
Ashley, K., (2008). *How Would Love Respond?: Imagine If You Were Given a Gift So Powerful That You Knew You Had to Share It With the World.* Dallas: BenBella Books.

SPECIAL EDITION for International Women's Day: Trailblazers pave the way for women
United Nations 2017, accessed 1 March 2016, http://www. un.org/en/events/womensday/

Acknowledgements – In Appreciation

Messages from the Heart has been two years in the making. A project like this doesn't happen in isolation – I am certainly not a one-woman band! There are plenty of people who have rallied around me to help produce this book and it is important that they know how thankful I am.

To Stephen and our children Leo and Eva – for allowing me to embrace my inner-writer and to accept that there's more to me than just being mum. You are my daily inspiration.

To Editor-In-Chief and the best mother-in-law anyone could ask for, Anne Halliday. You really helped me hone my craft. It is because of all our 'little' edits that would take a column from good to great. I love that 'we' never missed a deadline. I appreciate the time and energy you dedicated to this book.

To my mum, Jan Donges – obviously without you there would be no me, and without me there would be no *Messages from the Heart*! Thank you for always reassuring me to believe in myself and my dreams. Thank you especially for your help and support while I wrote the columns. No amount of gratitude can do your love justice.

To my dad, Lester Donges – from an early age you encouraged me to excel. Now, when I look at this book, I know that a lot of my drive and determination has come from you. This is a proud moment for both of us.

To my only sibling, my brother Stephen, thanks for being a good sport growing up with me as a big sister – I'm sure it has been character building! It's cool that my musical influence has resulted in you loving Guns n' Roses *almost* as much as I do.

To my grandparents, Gladys "Joyce" and Stan Donges who passed on a few years ago, I am forever thankful for your love and all the precious moments we shared. It is solely due to your legacy that I was able to self-publish this, my debut book. I couldn't think of a more fitting tribute. I know you are smiling down on me.

To the people who endorsed my book and wrote the most glowing comments about my writing from *their* hearts – Jodi Chapman, Dan Teck, Angela Boyle, Alex Kingsmill and the woman who started it all, Monique Patterson.

To Grace McClure – what a journey it has been! Thank you for kindly supporting me with your foreword and for always being a light on my path.

To Jane Caro for allowing me to grab a photo with you at Griffith's International Women's Day Breakfast in 2016. And most importantly for the message you wrote in your book, which I aim to uphold each day, and features in A Final Word.

To Kelly Dal Broi for taking the photo of Jane Caro and myself, and of course, for our first-class friendship.

To Chery Austen for your friendship, for being my "soft place to land" and the inspiration behind the quote in Column 23 (part one): Parenthood a constant juggling act.

To my best buddies Janelle De Frenza and Sally Giatras who share my positive vibe and just get me. Our friendship is authentic and enduring.

To my soul tribe, Vicki and Lionel Stewart, Noeline Smith, Donna Newton, Nina Ryan, Linda and Shirley Robb and Mandy Himsley – who lifted me up when I was down and who always cheered me on.

To all the friends and acquaintances who said, "I'll support you," "Good on you" or "I'll buy a copy of the book." Your words of encouragement always came at just the right time to help me stay motivated.

To Melissa Barton for capturing those beautiful moments with my daughter Eva for my suite of photographs, some of which are in this book.

To the team at the Griffith City Library, many of whom have become good friends. Thank you for all the times you allowed me to use the facilities and private rooms so I could work on my book in peace and quiet.

To Anne Barcelona, my Balboa Press consultant, for your patience, understanding and for answering all of my (sometimes tedious) questions so that this book would be the creation I envisaged.

To all the people who stopped me on the street or in the shops at Griffith and shared their responses to the columns – thank you. It really did give me the encouragement I needed for when the going got tough and the next weekly deadline loomed.

About the Author

Sharon Halliday is a columnist, Reiki practitioner, Angel Intuitive and mother. Two decades ago she discovered Louise Hay's book, *You Can Heal Your Life* and began learning about all things self-help. Sharon created her website and blog to inspire and empower others through her writing. Her posts are always topical and on trend – pop stars Iggy Azalea and Taylor Swift have even featured in her positive messages! Sharon's Facebook posts of her columns have been liked by popular self-help authors Colette Baron-Reid, Denise Linn, Cheryl Richardson and Dr John Gray.

In 2016, Sharon's writing was featured alongside bestselling authors Christine Arylo, Arielle Ford, and Kristine Carlson (of *Don't Sweat the Small Stuff*), plus a host of other international authors. The book, titled *365 Moments of Grace,* is now a #1 bestseller on Amazon in the U.S. and Canada.

In between parenthood and writing, Sharon sees clients in her Reiki and card reading practice, Healing from the Heart. This same business provided the perfect breeding ground of knowledge and experience for her to respond as Ask Sharon to the weekly questions submitted to *The Area News.*

Before her days as a columnist, Sharon completed a Bachelor of Tourism Degree, and won a host of accolades for her involvement in regional tourism. The award that got away was Cherry Queen (yes, it's a real thing) of her birthplace, the country town of Young. Sharon would instead settle for Runner-up. But all was made right in the world when in 2003 she was a recipient of the coveted Centenary Medal – awarded by the Australian Government for her contribution to Australian society.

While writing *Messages from the Heart*, Sharon resided in Griffith, regional New South Wales, Australia, but has since returned to Batemans Bay on the South Coast. She lives with her husband and two children. When Sharon's not writing, one of her favourite pastimes is to listen to the music of Guns n' Roses (which she says her obsession with borders on unhealthy!).

Connect with Sharon at: www.messagesfromtheheart.com.au or www.facebook.com.au/healingfromtheheartaustralia

Follow her on Twitter @SharonLHalliday

To enquire about having Sharon as a speaker for your next event, email her at: s_halliday@bigpond.com

Messages from the True Self

By Sharon Halliday

My true self does not know fear,
My true self does not know doubt,
My true self is not insecure,
My true self does not shout.

My true self does not judge,
My true self does not know sorrow,
My true self cherishes the present,
My true self believes in tomorrow.

My true self knows letting go,
My true self does not know pain,
My true self is guiding me,
My true self does not complain.

My true self is joy and peace,
My true self does not know spite,
My true self is all that is,
My true self is love and light.

Printed in the United States
By Bookmasters